Grammar Dimensions

Book 1A   **Second Edition**

Form, Meaning, and Use

Grammar Dimensions

BOOK 1A   SECOND EDITION

Form, Meaning, and Use

Diane Larsen-Freeman
Series Director

Victoria Badalamenti   Carolyn Henner Stanchina
LaGuardia Community College   Queens College
                City University of New York

Listening Activities in this text were developed by the editorial team
at Heinle & Heinle Publishers.

Heinle & Heinle Publishers
I(T)P An International Thomson Publishing Company

Pacific Grove • Albany • Bonn • Boston • Cincinnati • Detroit • London
Madrid • Melbourne • Mexico City • New York • Paris
San Francisco • Tokyo • Toronto • Washington

The publication of *Grammar Dimensions Book One*, Second Edition, was directed by members of the Newbury House ESL/EFL Team at Heinle & Heinle:

Erik Gundersen, Editorial Director
Bruno R. Paul, Market Development Director
Kristin M. Thalheimer, Production Services Coordinator
Nancy Mann Jordan, Developmental Editor
Stanley J. Galek, Vice President and Publisher

Also participating in the publication of this program were:

Project Manager/Desktop Pagination: Thompson Steele Production Services
Production Editor: Maryellen Eschmann Killeen
Manufacturing Coordinator: Mary Beth Hennebury
Associate Editor: Ken Pratt
Associate Market Development Director: Mary Sutton
Photo/Video Specialist: Jonathan Stark
Media Services Coordinator: Jerry Christopher
Interior Designer: Greta Sibley
Illustrators: Lyle Miller and Walter King
Photo Coordinator: Philippe Heckly
Cover Designer: Gina Petti, Rotunda Design
Cover Photo: Rowena Otremba, The Fringe

Heinle & Heinle Publishers is a division of International Thomson Publishing, Inc.

Manufactured in the United States of America

Library of Congress Cataloging-in-Publication Data

Badalamenti, Victoria.
      Grammar dimensions: Form, meaning, and use / Victoria Badalamenti, Carolyn Henner Stanchina;
Diane Larsen-Freeman, series director.
        p.   cm.
      Includes index.
      ISBN 0-8384-7154-4
      1. English language—Textbooks for foreign speakers. 2. English language—Grammar—Problems,
exercises, etc. I. Henner Stanchina, Carolyn. II. Larsen-Freeman, Diane. III. Title.
PE 1128, B233   1997
428.2'4—dc21   96-48584
                                                                              CIP

10 9 8 7 6 5 4 3

A Special Thanks

The series director, authors, and publisher would like to thank the following individuals who offered many helpful insights and suggestions for change throughout the development of *Grammar Dimensions, Second Edition.*

Jane Berger
Solano Community College, California

Mary Bottega
San Jose State University

Mary Brooks
Eastern Washington University

Christina Broucqsault
California State Polytechnic University

José Carmona
Hudson Community College

Susan Carnell
University of Texas at Arlington

Susana Christie
San Diego State University

Diana Christopher
Georgetown University

Gwendolyn Cooper
Rutgers University

Sue Cozzarelli
EF International, San Diego

Catherine Crystal
Laney College, California

Kevin Cross
University of San Francisco

Julie Damron
Interlink at Valparaiso University, Indiana

Glen Deckert
Eastern Michigan University

Eric Dwyer
University of Texas at Austin

Ann Eubank
Jefferson Community College

Alice Fine
UCLA Extension

Alicia Going
The English Language Study Center, Oregon

Molly Gould
University of Delaware

Maren M. Hargis
San Diego Mesa College

Mary Herbert
University of California, Davis Extension

Jane Hilbert
ELS Language Center, Florida International University

Eli Hinkel
Xavier University

Kathy Hitchcox
International English Institute, Fresno

Joyce Hutchings
Georgetown University

Heather Jeddy
Northern Virginia Community College

Judi Keen
University of California, Davis, and Sacramento City College

Karli Kelber
American Language Institute,
New York University

Anne Kornfeld
LaGuardia Community College

Kay Longmire
Interlink at Valparaiso University, Indiana

Robin Longshaw
Rhode Island School of Design

Bernadette McGlynn
ELS Language Center,
St. Joseph's University

Billy McGowan
Aspect International, Boston

Margaret Mehran
Queens College

Richard Moore
University of Washington

Karen Moreno
Teikyo Post University, Connecticut

Gino Muzzetti
Santa Rosa Junior College, California

Mary Nance-Tager
LaGuardia Community College,
City University of New York

Karen O'Neill
San Jose State University

Mary O'Neal
Northern Virginia Community College

Nancy Pagliara
Northern Virginia Community College

Keith Pharis
Southern Illinois University

Amy Parker
ELS Language Center, San Francisco

Margene Petersen
ELS Language Center, Philadelphia

Nancy Pfingstag
University of North Carolina, Charlotte

Sally Prieto
Grand Rapids Community College

India Plough
Michigan State University

Mostafa Rahbar
University of Tennessee at Knoxville

Dudley Reynolds
Indiana University

Ann Salzman
University of Illinois at Urbana-Champaign

Jennifer Schmidt
San Francisco State University

Cynthia Schuemann
Miami-Dade Community College

Jennifer Schultz
Golden Gate University, California

Mary Beth Selbo
Wright College, City Colleges of Chicago

Stephen Sheeran
Bishop's University, Lenoxville, Quebec

Kathy Sherak
San Francisco State University

Keith Smith
ELS Language Center, San Francisco

Helen Solorzano
Northeastern University

Book 1A Contents

(see page xii for Book 1B Contents)

UNIT 11   QUANTIFIERS

UNIT 12   ADVERBS OF MANNER

DIRECT AND INDIRECT OBJECTS, UNIT 13   OBJECT PRONOUNS

APPENDICES

1B Contents

UNIT 16   ADJECTIVE PHRASES

Another, The Other, Other(s), The Other(s), **Intensifiers**   239

UNIT 17   PAST TENSE OF BE

257

UNIT 18   PAST TENSE

269

From the Series Editor

To the Teacher

ABOUT THE SERIES

Grammar Dimensions, Second Edition is a comprehensive and dynamic, four-level series designed to introduce English-as-a-second or foreign language students to the form, meaning, and use of English grammatical structures with a communicative orientation. The series has been designed to meet the needs of students from the beginning to advanced levels and includes the following:

- *Grammar Dimensions, Book 1* ....beginning/high beginning
- *Grammar Dimensions, Book 2* ....intermediate
- *Grammar Dimensions, Book 3* ....high intermediate
- *Grammar Dimensions, Book 4* ....advanced

The textbooks are supplemented by workbooks, cassettes, instructor's manuals with tests, and a CD-ROM entitled *Grammar* 3D.

THE STORY OF GRAMMAR DIMENSIONS

Everywhere I went teachers would ask me, "What is the role of grammar in a communicative approach?" These teachers recognized the importance of teaching grammar, but they associated grammar with form and communication with meaning, and thus could not see how the two easily fit together.

Grammar Dimensions was created to help teachers and students appreciate the fact that grammar is not just about form. While grammar does indeed involve form, in order to communicate, language users also need to know what the forms mean and when to use them appropriately. In fact, it is sometimes learning the meaning or appropriate use of a particular grammar structure that represents the greatest long-term learning challenge for students, not learning to form it. For instance, learning when it is appropriate to use the present perfect tense instead of the past tense, or being able to use two-word or phrasal verbs meaningfully represent formidable learning challenges for ESL students.

The three dimensions of form, meaning and use can be depicted in a pie chart with their interrelationship illustrated by the three arrows:

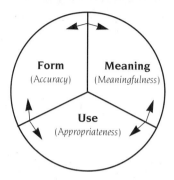

Helping students learn to use grammatical structures accurately, meaningfully, and appropriately is the fundamental goal of *Grammar Dimensions*. It is a goal consistent with the goal of helping students to communicate meaningfully in English, and one that recognizes the undeniable interdependence of grammar and communication.

ABOUT THE BOOKS

The books have been designed to allow teachers to tailor their syllabi for different groups of students. Some teachers have told us that they prefer to teach the units in a different order from that of the book. Teachers should feel free to do so or only to teach part of one unit and then return to do another part at a later time. Since the acquisition process is not a linear one (students do not completely master one structure before moving on to tackle another), teachers can construct syllabi which permit a recycling of material that causes their students difficulty. Of course, some teachers and students would rather use the book more conventionally, as well, by working their way through the units chronologically.

To allow for this possibility, some thought has been given to the sequencing of units within a book. The units have been ordered following different principles depending upon the level of the book. In Book 1, where students are introduced (or reintroduced in the case of false beginners) to basic sentence and subsentence grammatical structures and grammatical forms associated with semantic notions such as time and place, the units have been sequenced following conventional linguistic grading, building from one structure to the next. In Book 2, basic sentence and subsentence grammatical structures are dealt with once again. In addition, Book 2 also introduces language forms that support certain social functions such as making requests and seeking permission. At this level, units that share certain features have been clustered together. No more than three or four units are clustered at one time, however, in order to provide for some variety of focus. Although the four skills are dealt with in all of the books, the listening and speaking skills are especially prominent in Books 1 and 2.

Clustering 2-3 units that address related topics has been done for levels three and four as well. Book 3 deals with grammatical structures that ESL/EFL students often find challenging, such as the use of infinitives and gerunds. It also employs a discourse orientation when dealing with structures such as verb tenses and articles. Students learn how to use grammar structures accurately within contexts above the level of the single sentence. Book 4 deals with grammatical forms that are especially needed for academic and technical writing. It reveals to students the subtleties of certain grammatical structures and how they contribute to cohesion in discourse. Both books highlight the reading and writing skills and target structures for which students at these levels can benefit from special guidance in order to avoid their learning plateauing and their errors fossilizing.

ABOUT THE UNITS

Within a unit, the grammar structure is introduced to students within a communicative orientation. First, students have an opportunity to produce the target grammatical structures in a meaningful opening task. Thus, the grammar is contextualized and students are introduced to its meaning and use prior to any treatment of its form. Next, a series of alternating focus boxes and exercises presents students with the relevant form, meaning, and use facts concerning the target structure and provides practice with each. Finally, communication activities conclude each unit where students can more freely express themselves using the target grammar for communicative purposes. The following elaborates on this format.

Opening Task

In addition to providing a context for the meaningful use of the target grammar structures, the opening task serves several other purposes:

1. The tasks are motivating. Teachers tell us that students find the problem solving enjoyable and somewhat challenging.

2. Moreover, doing the task should activate the knowledge that students do have and help them recognize the need to learn the target structures they have not yet acquired.

3. Students' performance provides teachers with useful diagnostic information about where students' particular learning challenges lie. Thus, teachers can select material within a unit that has the most relevance for their students' learning needs.

Knowing their students' learning challenges helps teachers use their limited time more effectively. For instance, it may be the case that the students already know the target structure, in which case the unit may be skipped. It might also be that only the meaning or use of a particular structure is causing most students difficulty, in which case the focus boxes that deal with form issues can be ignored. Teachers are encouraged to see the book as a resource from which they can select units or parts of units that best meet their students' needs. (See the Instructor's Manual for tips on how to do this.)

Focus Boxes

The facts concerning the target structures are displayed in boxes clearly identified by the dimension(s) they address—form, meaning, or use. Each rule or explanation is preceded by examples. The examples, rules, and explanations are all arrayed in chart form for easy reference. Because the learning challenge presented by the three dimensions of language is not equal for all structures (for instance, some structures present more of a form-based challenge; for others the challenge is learning what the structures mean or when or why to use them), the number and foci of boxes differ from one unit to another.

Exercises

It is important to point out that it is not sufficient for students to know the rules or facts concerning these three dimensions. Thus, in *Grammar Dimensions*, we strive to have students develop the skill of "grammaring"—the ability to use structures accurately, meaningfully, and appropriately. To this end, the exercises are varied, thematically coherent, but purposeful. Often, students are asked to do something personally meaningful (e.g., students might be asked to register some opinion or to explain why they chose the answer that they did).

Activities

Located at the end of each unit, the communicative activities (purple pages) are designed to help students realize the communicative value of the grammar they are learning. As a complement to the meaningful task that opened the unit, grammar and communication are again practiced in tandem. Teachers, or students, may select from the ones offered those that they feel will be most enjoyable and beneficial.

NEW FEATURES IN THE SECOND EDITION

Teachers who have taught with *Grammar Dimensions* will note that the basic philosophy and approach to teaching grammar have not changed from the first edition. We believe they are still sound linguistically and pedagogically, and users of the first edition have confirmed this. However, our series users have also requested several new features, and modifications of others, and we have carefully woven these into this second edition:

1. One new feature that series users will notice is the incorporation of listening. Each unit has at least one activity in which students are asked to listen to a taped segment and respond in some way that involves the target structures.

2. A second new feature is the inclusion of a quiz after every unit to help teachers assess what students have learned from the unit. These 15-minute quizzes are available for duplication from the Instructor's Manuals.

3. Another change we have implemented is to streamline the grammar explanations and make them more user-friendly. You will notice that grammar terms are consistently labeled in the most straightforward and common manner. Also, note that, in each focus box, examples are consistently outlined on the left and explanations on the right to enhance clarity.

4. In response to user feedback, we have limited the texts to 25 units each. As was mentioned above, the material is meant to be used selectively, not comprehensively; still, some users preferred that the books have fewer units to begin with, and we agree that a reduced scope of grammatical topics in each book will help both teachers and students focus more successfully on their greatest learning challenges.

5. To honor the multiplicity of learning styles in the classroom and to capitalize on the dynamism of emerging technologies, we have developed a CD-ROM component called *Grammar* 3D to complement the *Grammar Dimensions* print materials. A wealth of exciting exercises and activities in *Grammar* 3D review and expand upon the lessons presented in the textbooks.

In all these ways, it is our hope that this series will provide teachers with the means to create, along with their students, learning opportunities that are tailored to students' needs, are enjoyable, and will maximize everyone's learning.

Diane Larsen-Freeman
School for International Training

OTHER COMPONENTS

In addition to the student text, each level of *Grammar Dimensions* includes the following components:

Audio Cassette

The audio cassette contains the listenings from the communicative activities (purple pages) in the student text.

An icon ✎ indicates which activities use the audio cassette.

Workbook

The Workbook provides additional exercises for each grammar point presented in the student text. Many of the workbook exercises are specially designed to help students prepare for the TOEFL® (Test of English as a Foreign Language).

Instructor's Manual

The Instructor's Manual contains:

- an introduction to philosophical background of the series
- general teaching guidelines
- unit-by-unit teaching notes
- student text answer key
- workbook answer key
- tapescript
- tests for each unit
- test answer key

CD-ROM

Grammar 3D is an ideal supplement to *Grammar Dimensions*. It provides comprehensive instruction and practice in 34 of the key grammar structures found in the text series.

Grammar 3D is appropriate for high-beginning to advanced students, and allows students to progress at their own pace. Students can access each grammar category at 3 or 4 levels of difficulty. They can then move to a lower level if they need basic review, or to a higher level for additional challenge.

An instructional "help page" allows students to access grammar explanations before they begin an exercise, or at any place within an exercise. Instruction is also provided through feedback that helps students understand their errors and guides them toward correct answers.

An icon indicates which focus boxes are supported by exercises in *Grammar* 3D.

To the Student

All grammar structures have a form, a meaning, and a use. We can show this with a pie chart:

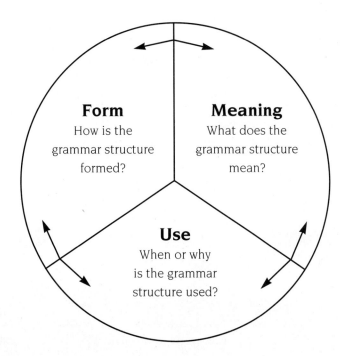

Often you will find that you know the answer to one or more of these questions, but not to all of them, for a particular grammar structure. This book has been written to help you learn answers to these questions for the major grammar structures of English. More importantly, it gives you practice with the answers so that you can develop your ability to use English grammar structures accurately, meaningfully, and appropriately.

At the beginning of each unit, you will be asked to work on an opening task. The task will introduce you to the grammar structures to be studied in the unit. However, it is not important at this point that you think about grammar. You should just do the task as well as you can.

In the next section of the unit are focus boxes and exercises. You will see that the boxes are labeled with FORM, MEANING, USE, or a combination of these, corresponding to the three parts of the pie chart. In each focus box is information that answers one or more of the questions in the pie. Along with the focus box are exercises that should help you put into practice what you have studied.

The last section of each unit contains communicative activities. Hopefully, you will enjoy doing these and at the same time receive further practice using the grammar structures in meaningful ways.

By working on the opening task, studying the focus boxes, doing the exercises, and engaging in the activities, you will develop greater knowledge of English grammar and skill in using it. I also believe you will enjoy the learning experience along the way.

Diane Larsen-Freeman
School for International Training

Acknowledgments

Series Director Acknowledgments

This edition would not have come about if it had not been for the enthusiastic response of teachers and students using the first edition. I am very grateful for the reception *Grammar Dimensions* has been given. By the same token, I want to give special thanks to those users who accepted our invitation to let us know how to better meet their needs with this second edition.

I am grateful for all the authors' efforts as well. To be a teacher, and at the same time a writer, is a difficult balance to achieve. So is being an innovative creator of materials, and yet, a team player. They have met these challenges exceedingly well in my opinion.

Then, too, the Heinle & Heinle team has been impressive. I am grateful for the leadership exercised first by Dave Lee, and later by Erik Gundersen. I also appreciate all the support from Ken Mattsson, Ken Pratt, Kristin Thalheimer, John McHugh, Bruno Paul, and Mary Sutton. Deserving special mention are Jean Bernard Johnston, and above all, Nancy Jordan, who never lost the vision while they attended to the detail with good humor and professionalism.

I have also benefited from the counsel of Marianne Celce-Murcia, consultant for this project, and my friend.

Finally, I wish to thank my family members, Elliott, Brent, and Gavin, for not once asking the (negative yes-no) question that must have occurred to them countless times: "Haven't you finished yet?"

Author Acknowledgments

This book is dedicated to Joel, Melanie, and Michele, who stood steadfastly by, tolerating all the moods and missed moments, as we reeled through this revision process. Their stamina was a great source of strength. This book also stands as an affirmation of the power of friendship; one solid enough to withstand the unspeakable frustrations and pressures of this process.

We are deeply grateful to Diane Larsen-Freeman for her patient guidance and supportive ear. Her intervention, on many occasions, allowed us to preserve the nature and original intent of this text.

We wish to extend our sincere thanks to the women at Thompson Steele Production Services, especially Marcia Croyle who, in the crunch, gave so generously of her time to try to set things right, and even saw the light regarding task-based, communicative grammar!

We also wish to thank both our ESL students at the City University of New York, and our Methods students at Queens College and The New School For Social Research, for their insights.

Finally, we credit Nancy Mann Jordan for her own personal vision and uncompromising efforts in bringing this project to fruition.

UNIT

1

The Verb Be
Affirmative Statements,
Subject Pronouns

Introductions

STEP ❶ Match the introductions to the pictures.

a.

b.

c.

d.

1. "Hello. My name is Monique. I'm French. I'm from Paris."

2. "I'm Chen. I'm Chinese. I'm from Beijing."

3. "I'm Fernando and this is Isabel. We are married. We are Colombian. We're from Bogota."

4. "Hi. I'm Genya. I'm Russian. I'm from Moscow."

1

STEP ❷ Look at Monique's information card. Then complete the information card about yourself. Introduce yourself to the class.

Information Card

Name: *Monique Delande*

Country: *France*

City: *Paris*

Nationality: *French*

Age: *28 years old*

Married/Divorced/Single: *single*

Information Card

Name: *Sachiko Okabe*

Country: *Japan*

City: *Tokyo*

Nationality: *Japan*

Age: *21*

Married/Divorced/Single: *single*

My name is *Sachiko Okabe*.

I am from *Japan*.

I'm *Japanese*.

I'm *21* years old.

I'm *single*.

>>>>>>>>>>>>>>>>>>>>>>>>> **FORM**

Be: Affirmative Statements

SUBJECT	VERB Be			
Monique She Paris	is		single. from Paris. in France.	singular
Fernando and Isabel They	are		Colombian. married.	plural

EXERCISE 1

Go back to the Opening Task on page 1. Underline all the singular subjects (one) and the verb *be*. Circle all plural subjects (more than one) and the verb *be*.

EXAMPLE: <u>My name is</u> Monique.

(We are) married.

EXERCISE 2

Fill in the blanks with the verb *be* or a name.

1. Genya _is_____ from Russia.

2. Isabel _____is_____ twenty-four years old.

3. _____Chen_____ is from the People's Republic of China.

4. Monique _____is_____ twenty-eight years old.

5. _Fernando and Isabel_ are married.

6. Chen _____is_____ twenty-five years old.

7. Genya _____was_____ divorced.

8. Fernando and Isabel _____are_____ Colombian.

9. Monique _____is_____ from France.

10. Moscow _____is_____ in Russia.

Fill in the blanks with *is* or *are* and the continents or regions.

Continents/Regions

Europe	Africa	The Caribbean
Central America	North America	South America
Asia	The Middle East	

1. Japan __is__ in __Asia__.

2. The Dominican Republic _____ in _____.

3. Senegal and Nigeria _____ in _____.

4. Honduras and El Salvador _____ in _____.

5. Peru and Ecuador _____ in _____.

6. Bangladesh _____ in _____.

7. Israel _____ in _____.

8. Canada _____ in _____.

9. Italy and Greece _____ in _____.

Now write two sentences of your own.

10. _____

11. _____

FOCUS 2 >>>>>>>>>>>>>> FORM/MEANING

Subject Pronouns with B*e*

SUBJECT PRONOUN	VERB B*e*	
I	am	single.
You	are	married.
He She It	is	Brazilian.
We You They	are	from Korea.

Note: Use subject pronouns only after you know the subject.
Chen is Chinese. He is from Beijing.

EXERCISE 4

Read the dialogues. Fill in the blanks with a subject pronoun.

EXAMPLE: __We__ are from the Dominican Republic.

1. A: _____ are from
    Wellington.

    B: _____ are from
    New Zealand. How interesting!

2. A: _____
    _____ Finnish.

    B: Yes, _____ is from
    Helsinki.

3. A: _____ are from
Argentina.

B: I know. _____ are stu-
dents in our class.

5. A: _____ are
Nigerian.

B: _____ are far from
home!

4. A: _____ is from
Berlin.

B: Oh, _____ is
German.

6. A: _____ am from
Florence.

B: Oh, _____ are
Italian.

EXERCISE 5

The subject pronouns in the sentences below are not correct. Circle the incorrect pronouns and write the correct sentences in the blanks.

1. Miyuki and Seung are from Asia. (You) are Asian. *They are Asian.*

2. John is thirty years old. She is from Cyprus. _____

3. You and Hamid are Algerian. They are from Algiers. _____

4. Port-au-Prince is in Haiti. She is the capital city. _____

5. Clemente and I are from Rome. They are Italian. _____

6. Pedro and Miguel are from Puebla. You are Mexican. _____

7. Ayelet and Amir are from Tel Aviv. We are Israeli. _____

Information Gap. Here are two lists of students in an English-as-a-Second-Language (ESL) class. Work with a partner. You look at List A and make a statement about student number 1 on your list. Your partner looks at List B on the next page and makes a second statement about student number 1 with a subject pronoun.

    EXAMPLE: You say: Mario is from Ecuador.

               Your partner says: He is Ecuadoran.

List A

Men	Country	Nationality
1. Mario	Ecuador	
2. Mohammed		Moroccan
3. Hideki and Yoshi	Japan	
4. Leonardo		Dominican
5. Oumar	Senegal	
Women		
6. Lilik		Indonesian
7. Krystyna	Poland	
8. Liisa and Katja		Finnish
9. Belen	Spain	
10. Margarita and Dalia		Brazilian

List B

Men	Country	Nationality
1. Mario		Ecuadoran
2. Mohammed	Morocco	
3. Hideki and Yoshi		Japanese
4. Leonardo	The Dominican Republic	
5. Oumar		Senegalese
Women		
6. Lilik	Indonesia	
7. Krystyna		Polish
8. Liisa and Katja	Finland	
9. Belen		Spanish
10. Margarita and Dalia	Brazil	

Make ten summary statements about the students in the ESL class in Exercise 6. Use the continents/regions.

EXAMPLES: Africa

Two students are from Africa. One is from Morocco and one is from Senegal.

1. Africa

   _____

2. Asia

   _____

3. Europe

   _____

4. Central America

   _____

5. South America

   _____

FOCUS 3 ➤➤➤➤➤➤➤➤➤➤➤➤➤➤➤➤➤➤➤➤➤➤➤ **FORM**

Contraction with *Be*

SUBJECT PRONOUN + *Be*		*Be* CONTRACTIONS	
I am		I'm	
You are		You're	
He is		He's	
She is	American.	She's	from the United States
It is		It's	
We are		We're	
You are		You're	
They are		They're	

EXERCISE 8

Think about the people and places in this unit. Match the people and places on the left with a letter on the right. Make two statements aloud. Use the name in the first statement and the subject pronoun and *Be* contraction in the second statement.

EXAMPLE: Genya is Russian. She's divorced.

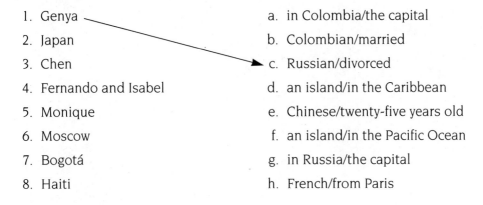

1. Genya
2. Japan
3. Chen
4. Fernando and Isabel
5. Monique
6. Moscow
7. Bogotá
8. Haiti

a. in Colombia/the capital
b. Colombian/married
c. Russian/divorced
d. an island/in the Caribbean
e. Chinese/twenty-five years old
f. an island/in the Pacific Ocean
g. in Russia/the capital
h. French/from Paris

Draw a line from the famous people on the left to the country they come from on the right. Fill in the nationality column on the right. Then tell the class what you know about the people.

EXAMPLE: Madonna is from the United States. She's American.

She's a pop music star.

Famous People	**Country**	**Nationality**
1. Madonna	France	1. _American_
2. Sophia Loren	South Africa	2. _____
3. Arnold Schwarzenegger	The United States	3. _____
4. The Rolling Stones	Great Britain	4. _____
5. Steffi Graff	Austria	5. _____
6. Michael Jordan	Germany	6. _____
7. Luciano Pavarotti	Brazil	7. _____
8. Catherine Deneuve	Italy	8. _____
9. Pele		9. _____
10. Nelson Mandela		10. _____

Introductions and Greetings

Introductions

EXAMPLES	EXPLANATIONS
(a) Hello. My name's Mario Ortiz. I'm from the Philippines	
(b) Hi! I'm Jennifer Brown. I'm from Florida. Please call me Jenny.	Introducing yourself
(c) Susan: Hello, John. This is Mario Ortiz. He's from the Philippines. John: Hi, Mario. Nice to meet you. Mario: Nice to meet you too, John.	Introducing another person
(d) Jeff: Hi, my name is Jeff Jones. I'm from California. What is your name? Alicia: Alicia Torres. Jeff: Where are you from, Alicia? Alicia: I'm from Chile. Jeff: Oh, really? Nice to meet you.	Meeting someone for the first time

Greetings

EXAMPLES	EXPLANATIONS
(e) Ms. Chen: Good morning, Mr. Brown. Mr. Brown: Good morning, Ms. Chen. How are you today? Ms. Chen: I'm fine, thank you. How are you? **(f)** Bill: Hello, Lautaro. How's everything? Lautaro: Fine thanks, Bill. And how are you? **(g)** Jake: Hi, Yoshi. How are you doing? Yoshi: O.K., Jake. How about you? Jake: Not bad.	Greetings can be formal or informal (very friendly). Formal Informal
(h) Hello, Ms. Smith. **(i)** NOT: Hello, Ms. Susan Smith. Hello, Ms. Susan.	Use a title (*Mr.*, *Ms.*, *Ms.*, *Dr.*, *Professor*) with a family name (last name), not with the full name, not with the first name.

EXERCISE 10

Introduce the person next to you to the class.

EXAMPLE: This is Yoshi. He's from Japan.

Fill in the blanks in the conversation.

EXAMPLE: Susan: I'm Susan Wilson from New York.

Jim: _Nice to meet you,_ Susan. _My name is_ Jim. _I'm_ from California.

1. **Fred:** Hello. I'm Fred.

   Phillippe: _____, Fred. _____ Phillippe.

2. **Lilik:** Hi! I'm Lilik. _____?

   Demos: My name's Demos.

   Lilik: _____?

   Demos: Greece. _____?

   Lilik: I'm from Indonesia.

3. **Michael:** Hi, Gregg. _____ Jane.

   Gregg: Hello, Jane. _____?

   Jane: Fine, thanks. _____?

   Gregg: Great!

Activities

Make a list of all the students in your class. Make a list of the countries they come from and their nationalities.

Names	Countries	Nationalities
_____	_____	_____
_____	_____	_____
_____	_____	_____
_____	_____	_____
_____	_____	_____

ACTIVITY 2

Write summary statements about the students in your class with the information from Activity 1.

EXAMPLE: Two students are Colombian.

Six students are from Asia.

ACTIVITY 3

On a piece of paper write three sentences about yourself. Do not write your name on the paper. Give the paper to your teacher. Your teacher reads each paper and the class guesses who the person is.

EXAMPLE: I am twenty-two years old. I'm from North Africa. I'm Algerian.

ACTIVITY 4

Work with a partner. Write information about yourself on a piece of paper. Exchange papers with your partner. Introduce your partner to the class.

EXAMPLE: This is Maria Gomez. She is from Mexico City. She is twenty-five years old. She is married.

ACTIVITY 5

Role-play with a partner.

1. You are a student and you greet your professor in school.

2. You greet your classmate.

ACTIVITY 6

Listen and decide. Three different people greet Mr. Maxwell Forbes, a bank manager, at a job interview. In two of the conversations, the greetings are wrong. Who gets the job? Circle the person who gets the job.

1. Mr. Blake   2. Ms. Robbins   3. Kevin Dobbs

UNIT

The Verb B*e*
Yes/No Questions, Be + Adjective, Negative Statements

OPENING TASK

Asking Personal Questions

Here are some advertisements from the newspaper. Match the questions below to the correct advertisers on the next page.

Are you single? Are you lonely? Are you ready to meet someone?
Call 1-800-555-LOVE

A.

Is English hard for you? Are verbs difficult? Are you unhappy about your pronunciation?
Enroll now! Call 555-4433

B.

Are you sad? Are you nervous? Are you worried?
Call 555-HELP

C.

Are you overweight? Are you out of shape? Is your body weak? Call now! 555-SLIM

D.

15

Dr. Friend, Psychiatrist   _____

The Lonely Hearts Dating Service   _____

New Body Health Club   _____

The Cool School of English   _____

Be: *Yes/No* Questions and Short Answers

YES/NO QUESTIONS	SHORT ANSWERS		
	AFFIRMATIVE		NEGATIVE CONTRACTIONS
(a) Am I overweight?	Yes,	you are.	No, you aren't. you're not.
(b) Are you nervous?		I am.	I'm not.
(c) Is he/she lonely?		he/she is.	he/she isn't. he's/she's not.
(d) Is English difficult?		it is.	it isn't. it's not.
(e) Are we out of shape?		you are.	you aren't. you're not.
(f) Are you single?		we are.	we aren't. we're not.
(g) Are verbs difficult?		they are.	they aren't. they're not.

EXERCISE 1

Ask your partner *yes/no* questions from the Opening Task on pages 15–16. Use short answers and contractions.

EXAMPLE: You: Are you single?

Your Partner: Yes, I am. OR No, I'm not.

EXERCISE 2

Read the conversations. Fill in the blanks with *yes/no* questions or short answers.

1. **A:** Hello, this is the New Body Health Club.

   B: Hello, _____ you open on Sunday?

A: Yes, _____ _____. We're open from seven in the morning until ten at night.

2. **Mitch:** Hello, my name is Mitch Brown. _____ you Karen Jones?

   Karen: Yes, _____ _____.

   Mitch: I got your telephone number from the Lonely Hearts Dating Service. How are you, Karen?

   Karen: Fine, thanks. And you?

   Mitch: Not bad, thanks. _____ _____ free tonight?

   Karen: No, I'm sorry, _____ _____. How about tomorrow?

   Mitch: Great!

3. **A:** Hello, is this Dr. Friend's office?

   B: Yes, _____ _____.

   A: _____ Dr. Friend busy? I need to speak to him.

   B: Just a minute, please.

4. **Secretary:** Cool School of English. May I help you?

   Hui Chen: Yes, I'd like some information about your classes, please.

   Secretary: Of course.

   Hui Chen: _____ the classes big?

   Secretary: No, _____ _____. We have only ten people in a class.

   Hui Chen: _____ the teachers good?

   Secretary: Yes, _____ _____. All the teachers are excellent.

   Hui Chen: _____ the tuition expensive?

   Secretary: No, _____ _____. It's only $800 for ten weeks.

   Hui Chen: O.K. Thank you very much.

   Secretary: You're welcome. Goodbye.

FOCUS 2 >>>>>>>>>>>>>>>>>>>>>>>>> FORM

Be + Adjective

EXAMPLES	EXPLANATIONS
(a) Dr. Friend is **busy.** **(b)** The health club is **open.** **(c)** Verbs are **difficult.**	An adjective describes a person, place, or thing. Adjectives can come after the verb *be*.
(d) They are **excellent.** **(e)** NOT: They are excellents.	Do not put "s" on the adjective when the subject is plural (more than one).
(f) The classes are **very good.**	*Very* makes the adjective stronger. *Very* comes before an adjective.

EXERCISE 3

Go back to the Opening Task on page 15 and circle all the adjectives.

EXAMPLE: Are you (single)? Are you (lonely)?

EXERCISE 4

Work with a partner. Ask your partner questions about the pictures. Use the adjectives in parentheses. Your partner finds the opposites of each adjective from the box at the bottom of the next page and answers your questions.

Is he young?
No, he isn't.
He's old.

Example: (young)

1. (sad)

2. (weak)

3. (thin)

The Verb Be   **19**

4. (rich)

5. (neat)

6. (short)

7. (serious)

8. (calm)

9. (healthy)

10. (energetic)

Opposites					
funny	sick	lazy	happy	poor	nervous
old	strong	overweight	tall	messy	

Mark Heller is single and lonely. He wants a girlfriend. He puts this advertisement in the newspaper. Fill in the blanks with *am* or *are*. Use contractions where possible.

1) I'm _____ 28 years old. (2) I _____ 6'2" tall. (3) I _____ single. (4) I _____ handsome and athletic. (5) I _____ romantic. (6) I _____ (negative) shy. (7) _____ you under 30? (8) _____ you tall? (9) _____ you outgoing? (10) _____ you ready for marriage? Then call me: (718) 555-7954.

Information gap. Three women answer Mark's advertisement. Work with a partner. You look at Chart A and your partner looks at Chart B on page E-1. Ask each other *yes/no* questions to find the information that you do not have in your chart. Then put a check in the correct place.

EXAMPLE: You: Is Shelley tall?

Your Partner: No, she isn't.

You: Is she average height?

Your Partner: Yes, she is.

Chart A

Name: Age:	Cindy 22	Shelley 27	Gloria 30
1. Height			
tall			
average height			✔
short	✔		
2. Weight			
thin			
average weight			✔
overweight		✔	

3. Personality	Cindy	Shelley	Gloria
shy			
friendly	✔		✔
quiet			
talkative	✔		✔
neat			
messy	✔		
funny	✔		
serious			
nervous	✔		
calm			✔

EXERCISE 7

Ask a partner questions with the adjectives below.

young	funny	tall	strong	serious	healthy
energetic	calm	neat	lazy	messy	rich

EXAMPLE: You: Are you tall?

Your Partner: Yes, I am. OR No, I'm not.

EXERCISE 8

Write five statements about what you **like** about your partner.

EXAMPLE: _My partner is funny. He's energetic._

_____

_____

_____

_____

_____

FOCUS 3 ➤➤➤➤➤➤➤➤➤➤➤➤➤➤➤➤➤➤➤ FORM/USE

Be: Negative Statements and Contractions

NEGATIVE STATEMENT	CONTRACTION OF SUBJECT + Be	CONTRACTION OF Be + NOT
I am not shy.	I'm not shy.	*
You are not old.	You're not old.	You aren't old.
He She } is not ready. It	He's She's } not ready. It's	He She } isn't ready. It
We You } are not nervous. They	We're You 're } not nervous. They're	We You } aren't nervous. They

Note: The contraction of *be* followed by *not* (*he's not*) makes a negative statement stronger than a negative contraction (*he isn't*).

Read the statements below each ID (Identification) card. If the information is correct, say "That's right." If the information is not correct, make a negative statement with a *be* contraction + *not* and a correct affirmative statement.

EXAMPLE: 1. His last name is Yu-ho.

His last name's not Yu-ho.

It's Oh.

Last Name:	*Oh*
First Name:	*Yu-ho*
Country:	*Taiwan*
Nationality:	*Taiwanese*
Age:	23
Marital Status:	*single*

Last Name:	*Ryperman*
First Name:	*Aline*
Country:	*Holland*
Nationality:	*Dutch*
Age:	32
Marital Status:	*married*

1. His last name is Yu-ho.

2. He is Korean.

3. He's twenty-five.

4. He's single.

5. Her first name is Alice.

6. She is Dutch.

7. She's from Germany.

8. She's fifty-two.

Last Name:	*Mafegna*
First Name:	*Abiy*
Country:	*Ethiopia*
Nationality:	*Ethiopian*
Age:	30
Marital Status:	*single*

Last Name:	*Shram*
First Name:	*Jehad*
Country:	*Lebanon*
Nationality:	*Lebanese*
Age:	27
Marital Status:	*single*

9. His first name is Mafegna.

10. He's Indian.

11. He's thirty.

12. He's married.

13. Jehad is Jordanian.

14. He is twenty-nine.

15. He's single.

Complete each dialogue with an affirmative or a negative statement and an adjective from the list below.

Adjectives:					
delicious	smart	ugly	beautiful	selfish	mean

1. **Ann:** I'm short. I (a) _____ fat.
   I (b) _____ ugly.

   Marilyn: No, you (c) _____ .
   You (d) _____ , Ann!

2. **Woman:** This dinner is terrible! I'm sorry.

   Guest: No, it (a) _____ .
   It's (b) _____ !

3. **Mike:** I (a) _____ nervous about this
   test. I (b) _____ stupid, Sam!

   Sam: No, you (c) _____ , Mike.
   You (d) _____ ! Your average is 98!

4. **Sally:** You know Jill, I'm in love with Jack. He (a)
   _____ kind and generous.

   Jill: Kind and generous??? No, he (b)

   _____ .

   He (c) _____ .

5. **Salesperson:** That dress is perfect on you.

   Customer: Perfect? Oh no, it (a) _____ .
   It (b) _____ .

Activities

Work with a partner. Make true statements with the subjects and adjectives below. Use the affirmative or negative form of the verb *be*. The pair with the most correct sentences wins.

EXAMPLE: The President is not tall.

Subject	Be	Adjective
My country		happy
I		single
My classmate		tall
The President		delicious
The United States		old
My friends		beautiful
My father		smart
English		big
Roses		important
		expensive

ACTIVITY 2

STEP ❶ Check all the adjectives that describe you.

Adjective	Column A: You	Column B: Your Partner
shy		
quiet		
talkative		
romantic		
practical		
athletic		
lazy		
healthy		
funny		
friendly		
messy		
serious		

STEP ❷ Ask your partner *yes/no* questions with the adjectives in the box. Check the adjectives in Column B.

> **EXAMPLE: You ask:** Are you shy?
>
> **Your partner answers:** Yes, I am. OR No, I'm not.

STEP ❸ Write three ways you and your partner are similar and three ways you are different.

> **EXAMPLE:** Similar

1.	We are athletic.
2.	We are healthy.

Different

1.	My partner is romantic
	I'm practical.
2.	He's serious. I'm funny.

ACTIVITY 3

Write your own personal advertisement for the newspaper or write one for a friend who is single.

> **EXAMPLE:** My name is (1) _____.
>
> I'm (2) _____ (nationality).
>
> I'm (3) _____ years old.
>
> I'm (4) _____ (adjective).
>
> I'm (5) _____ (adjective).
>
> And I'm (6) _____ (adjective).
>
> Are you (7) _____ (adjective)?
>
> Are you (8) _____ (adjective)?
>
> PLEASE CALL ME!

Look at your answers to Exercise 6. Who is the best woman for Mark? Discuss your answers.

STEP ❶ Consuela is at the Cool School of English to register for classes. Listen to the conversation and look at the questions below. Check Yes or No.

	Yes	No
1. Is Consuela a new student?		
2. Is Consuela an intermediate-level student?		
3. Is Consuela interested in morning classes?		

STEP ❷ With a partner, ask and answer the questions. If the answer is no, make a true statement.

STEP ❸ Role-play the conversation.

The Verb Be
Wh-Question Words, Prepositions of Location

Test Your World Knowledge

STEP ❶ Match the questions with the answers.

Questions	Answers
b 1. What's the Amazon?	a. the Pope
e 2. Where is the Kremlin?	b. It's a river.
a 3. Who is the head of the Catholic Church?	c. It's 12:00 noon.
f 4. How is the weather in Argentina in June?	d. about 4,700 years old
j 5. Where are the Himalayas?	e. in Moscow
i 6. When is Thanksgiving in the United States?	f. It's cold.
c 7. It's 9 A.M.* in California. What time is it in New York?	g. North America, South America, Africa, Asia, Australia, Europe, and Antarctica
d 8. How old are the Pyramids in Egypt?	h. because it is Independence Day
g 9. What are the names of the seven continents?	i. the last Thursday in November
h 10. Why is July 4th special in the United States?	j. in India, Nepal, and Tibet

*A.M.: in the morning

STEP ❷ Make up two questions of your own. Ask your classmates the questions.

Wh-Question Words with Be

Wh-question words are: *what, where, who, when, how, what time, how old,* and *why.*
Use Wh-question words to ask for specific information.

QUESTION WORD	Be	SUBJECT	ANSWER	MEANING
What	is 's	the Amazon?	a river	THING
Where	are	the Himalayas?	in India, Nepal, or Tibet	PLACE
Who	is 's	the head of the Catholic Church?	the Pope	PEOPLE
How	is 's	the weather in Argentina in June?	It's cold.	CONDITIONS
When	is 's	Thanksgiving in the United States?	the last Thursday in November	TIME
What time	is	it in New York?	It's 12:00.	TIME ON A CLOCK
How old	are	the Pyramids in Egypt?	about 4,700 years old	AGE
Why	is 's	July 4th special in the United States?	because it is Independence Day	REASON

Fill in the blanks with one of these *wh*-question words: *what, where, how, how old, what time,* and *why.*   when

Questions	Answers
1. ___How old___ is the Great Wall of China?	about 2,200 years old
2. ___Who___ are the authors of *Grammar Dimensions,* Book I?	Victoria Badalamenti and Carolyn Henner Stanchina.
3. ___Where___ is Morocco?	in Africa
4. ___How___ is the weather in the summer in Washington, D.C.?	It's hot.
5. ~~Where~~ What is the capital of Belgium? Country	Brussels.
6. ___When time___ is the first day of summer?	June 21st.
7. It's 10 A.M.* in Boston. ___What time___ is it in Paris?	It's 4:00 P.M.*
8. ___When___ is Independence Day in France?	July 14th.
9. ~~What~~ why are you in this class?	to learn English
10. ___What___ are the Nile and the Mississippi?	rivers

*A.M. = morning
*P.M. = afternoon, evening, night

July, 20 Home work

Match the question in Column A to the answer in Column B. Write the letter in the blank on the left.

	Column A	**Column B**
d	1. What's your name?	a. October 17th.
h	2. Where are you from?	b. I'm Turkish.
e	3. Where is Istanbul?	c. To study English.
b	4. What's your nationality?	d. Mehmet.
f	5. How old are you?	e. It's in Turkey.
a	6. When's your birthday?	f. Twenty-five.
c	7. Why are you here?	g. Fine, thanks.
g	8. How are you?	h. Istanbul.

Write questions with *wh*-question words for these answers.

1. _What time is it?_ ?

   It's 10:15 right now.

2. _What day is it_ ?

   It's Monday.

3. _What's your name_ ?

   My name is Berta.

4. _How old are you_ ?

   I'm twenty-five years old.

5. _When's your birthday_ ?

   My birthday is July 15th.

6. _What's your nationality_ ?

   I'm Mexican.

7. _What is your hometown / Where do you live_ ?

   My hometown is Mexico City.

8. _Wher are your family / Where do your family live_ ?

   My family is in Mexico City.

verb → do (I do / You do / they do it he/she) does

The Verb Be   **33**

9. _____How is the weather in Maxico City_____?

The weather in Mexico City is hot.

10. _____Why are you here_____?

I am here to study English.

Work with a partner. Ask your partner the same questions for Exercise 2 above.

EXERCISE 4

Write five questions about students in the class with the question word *Who*. Then ask your partner the questions.

EXAMPLE: Who is from Asia?

Who is twenty-five years old?

Who is tall?

FOCUS 2 >>>>>>>>>>>>>>>>>>>>>>>>>> **USE**

How to Ask Questions about English

When you need to ask about a word in English, you say:

(a) **What** is the meaning of *crowded*?

(b) **What** is the spelling of *crowded*?

(c) **What** is the pronunciation of *c-r-o-w-d-e-d*?

EXERCISE 5

Read the paragraph below about Vancouver. Underline the words you don't know or can't pronounce. Ask your teacher or classmates questions.

EXAMPLE: What is the meaning of <u>crowded</u>?

Vancouver is a city in Canada. It's on the Pacific coast. The city is magnificent. It is clean and open. It isn't <u>crowded</u>. Almost three-quarters of the population are of British ancestry. Other ethnic groups are the Chinese, French, Japanese, and East Indians. As a result, the food in Vancouver is varied and delicious. It is a wonderful place for a vacation.

Using It to Talk about the Weather

QUESTIONS	ANSWERS		
How's the weather in New York?	**It's** sunny **It's** hot	in the	summer.
	It's cold **It's** snowy		winter.
	It's cloudy **It's** rainy		spring.
	It's windy **It's** cool		fall.
What's the temperature today?	**It's** 77 degrees Fahrenheit/25 degrees Celsius.		

Work with a partner. You look at Map A and your partner looks at Map B (on page E-2). You have some information about the weather in the different cities in Map A. Your partner has other information in Map B. Ask each other questions to find out the missing information.

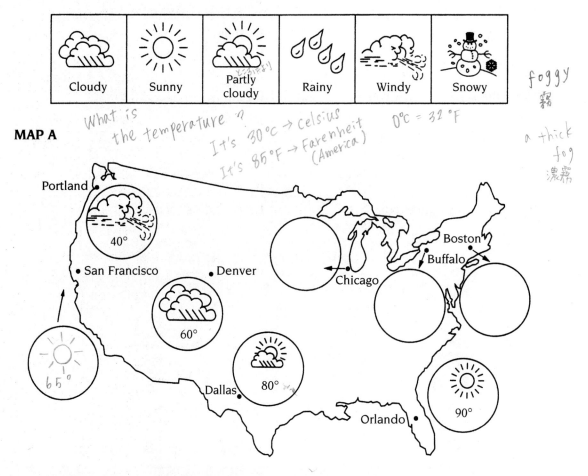

Cloudy	Sunny	Partly cloudy	Rainy	Windy	Snowy

foggy
霧

a thick
fog
濃霧

MAP A

What is the temperature?
It's 30°C → Celsius
It's 85°F → Farenheit (America)
0°C = 32 °F

Portland 40°

San Francisco

Denver 60°

Chicago

Boston

Buffalo

65°

Dallas 80°

Orlando 90°

EXAMPLE: **You:** How's the weather in San Francisco today?

Your Partner: It's sunny.

You: What's the temperature?

°C × 2 ≠ 28 = °F   *1.8*

Your Partner: It's 65 degrees.

時差「Brazil is 1 hour ahead
time (different) 後
Vancouver is 3 hours behind 前

Japan is ahead of Canada

FOCUS 4 >>>>>>>>>>>>>>>>>>>>>>>>>>>> **USE**

Using *It* to Talk about Time

WHAT TIME IS IT? / What's the time?

3:00	**It's** three o'clock. **It's** three.	
3:05	**It's** five after three. *five past three* *three - o - five* < 3 0 5 >	
3:15 15 mins = 1/4 of 1 hour (25¢ = 1/4 of $1 quarter)	**It's** three-fifteen. **It's** a quarter past three. **It's** a quarter after three.	
3:30	**It's** three-thirty. **It's** half past three.	
3:45	**It's** three forty-five. **It's** a quarter to four.	

7 pm ,   7:30 pm

ゼロ オー
0 → 0

military time
16:00 six hundred
23:58 twenty-three

3:50	**It's** three-fifty. **It's** ten to four.	(clock showing 3:50)
12:00	**It's** twelve o'clock. **It's** noon. **It's** midnight.	(clock showing 12:00)

EXERCISE 7

Work with a partner. You say the time one way. Your partner says the time a different way.

EXAMPLE: 6:30

It's six thirty.

It's half past six.

1. 8:15	2. 5:20	3. 7:35	4. 9:45	5. 11:30
6. 1:55	7. 3:10	8. 2:40	9. 4:10	

Look at the map of the time zones in the United States. Ask and answer the questions.

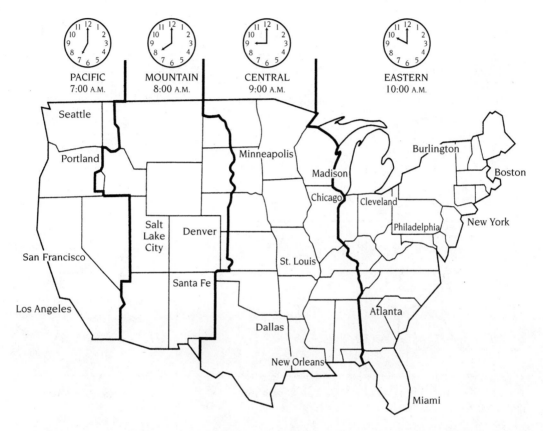

1. It's 7:00 A.M. in San Francisco. What time is it in New York? _It's 10:00 A.M_.

2. It's 10:45 P.M. in Miami. What time is it in Salt Lake City? _It's 8:45 PM_.

3. It's 6:50 P.M. in Minneapolis. What time is it in New Orleans? _It's 6:50 P.M_.

4. It's 10:30 P.M. in Santa Fe. What time is it in Chicago? _It's 11:30 P.M_.

5. It's 2:15 A.M. in Los Angeles. What time is it in Boston? _It's 5:15 AM_.

6. It's 9:10 A.M. in Dallas. What time is it in Portland? _It's 7:10 AM_.

7. It's 10:20 A.M. in Atlanta. What time is it in Denver? _It's 8:20 A.M_.

8. It's 10:05 A.M. in Seattle. What time is it in Atlanta? _It's 1:05 P.M_.

Now make five questions of your own for your partner to answer.

Prepositions of Location

Prepositions of location tell where something is.

COMMON PREPOSITIONS OF LOCATION

The ball is **in** the box.	The ball is **on** the box.	The ball is **above** the box.
The ball is **next to** the box.	The ball is **in back of** the box.	The ball is **under** the box.
The ball is **near** the box. It isn't next to the box.	The ball is **behind** the box.	The ball is **opposite** the box.
The ball is **between** the two boxes.	The ball is **in front of** the box.	

SUBJECT +	Be +	PREPOSITIONAL PHRASE (PREPOSITION + NOUN)
Prague	is	**in** the Czech Republic.
It	's	**on** the Vultava River.
The hotel	is	**near** the Vultava River.

EXERCISE 9

Sally and her family are in Prague, in the Czech Republic. Read the postcard and circle the prepositions of location.

postcard

Hi everybody. Here we are in Prague, the capital city of the Czech Republic. It is a beautiful city in Central Europe. I am between Ken and Jirka, our Czech friend. In this photo, we are at a cafe next to the Charles Bridge. Michele is behind me—she's camera shy! And right opposite the cafe is a souvenir shop. Prague is very popular in the summer. Many tourists come here to visit. The couple next to us is from Italy. They love Prague too!

Information Gap. You cannot find items 1–6 in Picture A. Your partner cannot find items 7–12 in Picture B on page E-3. Ask each other questions with *where*.

EXAMPLE: Student A asks: Where are my slippers?

Student B says: They're under the sofa. / It's

PICTURE A

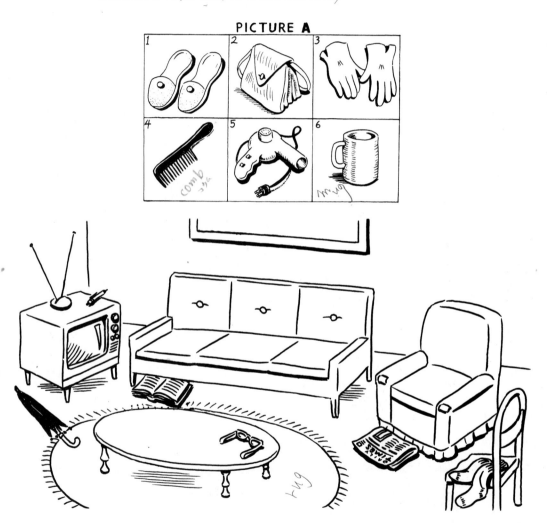

This is a map of your neighborhood. The names of the places are missing. Read the sentences and fill in the names of the places on the map.

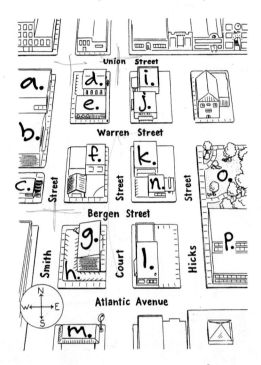

1. The park is on the corner of Hicks and Warren Street. O
2. The hospital is next to the park. P
3. The bank is on the southwest corner of Court Street and Union. d
4. The drugstore is next to the bank. e
5. The liquor store is across the street from the drug store on Court Street. j
6. The video store is near the liquor store. i
7. The movie theater is on the west side of Court Street between Bergen and Atlantic. g
8. The parking lot is behind the movie theater. h
9. The bakery is across the street from the movie theater. l
10. The gas station is on the corner of Hicks and Bergen. n
11. The hardware store is on the southeast corner of Court Street and Warren. K
12. The bookstore is opposite the hardware store. f
13. The newsstand is on the corner of Bergen and Smith Streets. c
14. The pet store is on the southwest corner of Union Street and Smith Street. a
15. The supermarket is between the pet store and the newsstand on Smith Street. b
16. The diner is on Atlantic Avenue. m

Activities

TEST YOUR KNOWLEDGE GAME

Get into two teams.

STEP ❶ Team 1 chooses a category and an amount of money. Team 2 asks a question with *what* or *where*. If Team 1 answers correctly, they get the money.

STEP ❷ Team 2 chooses a category and an amount of money. Team 1 asks a question with *what* or *where*. If Team 2 answers correctly, they get the money. The team with the most money at the end wins.

EXAMPLES: **Step 1.**

Team 1: Monuments for $30.

Team 2: Where is the Colosseum?

Team 1: It's in Rome, Italy.

			Categories		
Amount $$$	Monuments	Capitals	Countries	Continents	Rivers, Mountains, Deserts
Question	Where is/ are	What's the capital of	Where's	Where's	Where is/ are
$10	The Eiffel Tower	Afghanistan	Managua	Canada	The Sahara Desert
$20	The Great Wall	Greece	Nagasaki	Chile	The Rocky Mountains
$30	The Colosseum	Israel	Budapest	India	The Amazon River
$40	The Pyramids	Peru	Capetown	Egypt	Mt. Everest
$50	The Taj Mahal	Turkey	Zurich	Portugal	The Nile River

! exprmation point . ? question mark . period

ACTIVITY 2

Ask a classmate about his or her hometown. Ask questions with *is/are* . . . or *wh*-question words.

EXAMPLE: You: Where are you from? **Your Partner:** Acapulco.

Where's Acapulco? It's in Mexico.

How is the weather? It's hot in the summer and mild in the winter.

Are the people friendly? Yes, they are.

The words in the box will help you:

What place is famous in your city?

Weather	People	Other *Is it ?*
hot	happy	expensive
warm	friendly	cheap
mild	hard-working	small
cold	cold	big
sunny	religious	crowded ↔ *not busy*
dry	outgoing	delicious ↔ *terrible/awful*
humid	quiet	safe
rainy	rich	dangerous
cloudy	poor	clean

How's the food?
It's delicious.

(it)
Is your city crowded?

ACTIVITY 3

Write about your partner's hometown.

EXAMPLE: *My classmate is from Mexico City. Mexico City is the capital of Mexico. Mexico City is big. It is crowded. It is hot in the summer. People are friendly. The food is delicious.*

ACTIVITY 4

Draw a map of your hometown or the place where you live now. Describe your map to your partner. Then write down the description, using prepositions.

EXAMPLES: *This is my house. It's on Main Street. The drugstore is on the corner of Main and 1st Avenue. The supermarket is opposite the drugstore.*

ACTIVITY 5

Listen to the telephone conversation between a student and a secretary at a college. Fill in the following places on the campus map:

- Parking B, アドミニ ストレション 応接係
- Administration Building
- library
- bookstore

- English as a Second Language Department
- auditorium — ホール 八千青館
- cafeteria

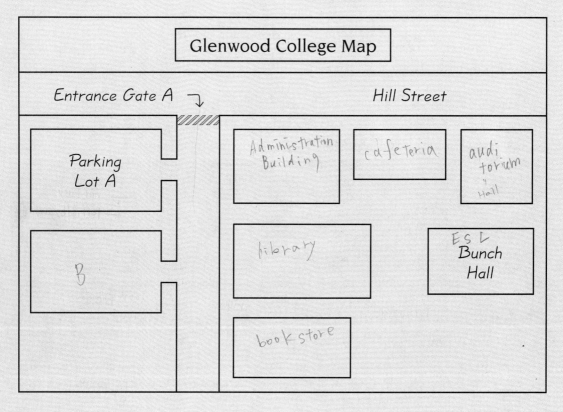

Glenwood College Map

Entrance Gate A

Hill Street

Parking Lot A

B

Administration Building

cafeteria

audi torium " Hall

library

 E S L Bunch Hall

book store

What time did you wake up?

Nouns
Count and Noncount Nouns, Be + Adjective + Noun

Categories

STEP ❶ Write each word in the box in one of the three circles below.

milk	dresses	cash
dollars	bread	a shoe
a shirt	cents	an egg

Category

1. Food

an egg
bread
milk

3. Money

dollars
cents
cash

2. Clothing

a shirt
dresses
a shoe

STEP ❷ Look at the same words in different groups. What are the categories? Write a name for each category.

Category

1. _*count*_

a shirt
a shoe
an egg

3. _*Non count*_

milk
bread
cash

2. _*count*_

dollars
cents
dresses

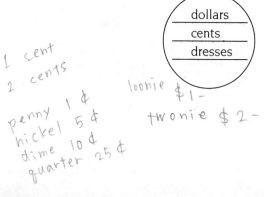

1 cent
2 cents

penny 1¢
nickel 5¢
dime 10¢
quarter 25¢

loonie $1 -
twonie $2 -

Count Nouns and Noncount Nouns

person → Val
place → Las Vegas
thing → dog, chair, car.

Cash

Coins

We can see things as whole or as things we can count. We use noncount nouns like *cash* when we see a thing as whole. We use count nouns like *coins* when we refer to things we can count.

EXAMPLES	EXPLANATIONS
Count Nouns SINGULAR → 1 PLURAL → *more than 1* a dress dresses an egg eggs	**Things we can count** Count nouns take *a/an* in the singular. They take *-s* or *-es* in the plural.
Noncount Nouns → *same singlar + plural* money *tea* cash *fish* clothing	**Things we don't count** Noncount nouns have one form. They are not singular or plural.

EXERCISE 1

Look at the list of words from the Opening Task. Check count or noncount.

home work

	Count Noun	**Noncount Noun**
food	*foods*	
milk		*milk*
egg	*eggs*	
bread		*bread*
clothing		*clothing*
dresses	*dresses*	
shirt	*shirts*	

	Count Noun	Noncount Noun
shoe	shoes	
money		money
dollars	dollars	
cents	cents	
cash		cash

FOCUS 2 ▷▷▷▷▷▷▷▷▷▷▷▷▷▷▷▷▷▷▷▷▷▷▷ FORM

A/An with Singular Count Nouns

A	AN
a house **a** movie **a** uniform*	**an** orange **an** egg **an** hour*
Use *a* before a word beginning with a consonant or a consonant sound. *uniform begins with a vowel but has the consonant sound of "y" as in *you*.	Use *an* before a word beginning with a vowel (a, e, i, o, u) or a vowel sound. *hour begins with a consonant but the "h" is silent.

EXERCISE 2

List the words below under the correct categories. Then, read your lists to your partner with *a* or *an*.

earring	bed	watch	necklace
dormitory	table	apple	house
orange	apartment	ring	desk
armchair	banana	pear	hotel

Fruit	**Furniture**	**Jewelry**	**Housing**
an orange	a bed	an earring	a domitory
an apple	a table	a necklace	a house
a pear	a desk	a ring	an apartment
a banana	an armchair	a watch	a hotel

EXERCISE 3

For each picture write a sentence to show the person's occupation. Use *a/an*.

EXAMPLES:

He's a waiter.

She's an athlete.

1. actor

    He's an actor.

2. secretary

    セクレタリー

    She's a secretary

3. dentist   _He's a dentist_

4. cashier   _She's a cashier._

5. flight attendant   _He's a flight attendant._

6. doctor   _He's a doctor_

7. nurse   _He's a nurse_

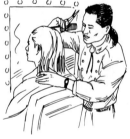

8. hairdresser   _He's a hairdresser_

9. engineer   _She's an engineer._

10. accountant   _She's an accountant._

52   Unit 4

Test your knowledge. Work with a partner. You read the question on the left. Your partner finds the answer on the right and reads it using *a/an*.

EXAMPLE: You: What's Poland?

Your Partner: (m) It's a country.

m 1. What's Poland?

g 2. What is Thanksgiving?

j 3. What is the Atlantic?

f 4. What is Puerto Rico?

n 5. What's the Sahara?

a 6. What is Africa?

k 7. What's New York?

l 8. What's the Concorde?

d 9. What's Big Ben?

h 10. What is the Louvre?

i 11. What is Harvard?

c 12. What's sixty minutes?

b 13. What's a Mercedes?

e 14. What's the Amazon?

a. It's _____ a _____ continent.

b. It's _____ a _____ car.

c. It's _____ an _____ hour

d. It's _____ a _____ clock.

e. It's _____ a _____ river.

f. It's _____ an _____ island.

g. It's _____ a _____ holiday in the United States and Canada.

h. It's _____ a _____ museum.

i. It's _____ a _____ university.

j. It's _____ an _____ ocean.

k. It's _____ a _____ city.

l. It's _____ an _____ airplane.

m. It's _____ a _____ country.

n. It's _____ a _____ desert.

Spelling of Regular Plural Count Nouns

SINGULAR	PLURAL	EXPLANATIONS
(a) a car a book	two cars three books	To make the plural form of most count nouns, add -s.
(b) a boy a radio	four boys two radios	Nouns that end in: vowel + *y* vowel + *o* Plural form: add -s.
(c) a class a sandwich a dish a box	two classes two sandwiches two dishes three boxes	Nouns that end in: *ss* *ch* *sh* *x* Plural form: add -es.
(d) a potato a tomato	six potatoes four tomatoes	Nouns that end in: consonant + *o* Plural form: add -es.
(e) a baby a city	babies cities	Nouns that end in: consonant + *y* Plural form: change *y* to *i*, add -es.
(f) a thief a life	two thieves three lives	Nouns that end in: *f* or *fe* Plural form: change *f* to *v*, add -es. Exceptions: *chief—chiefs* *chef—chefs*

Write the plural form of the words below.

1. party _parties_
2. shoe _shoes_
3. fox _foxes_
4. dictionary _dictionaries_
5. week _weeks_
6. glass _glasses_

7. wife _wives_
8. watch _watches_
9. leaf _leaves_
10. lady _ladies_
11. month _months_
12. key _keys_   (e i e) X

Complete the sentences with the plural of one of the nouns below.

city	story	holiday	university	state
mountain	country	continent	company	ocean

1. Thanksgiving and Christmas are _holidays_ .
2. The Atlantic and the Pacific are _oceans_ .
3. Africa and Asia are _continents_ .
4. Harvard and Yale are _universities_ .
5. IBM and Sony are _companies_ .
6. "Cinderella" and "Beauty and the Beast" are _stories_ .
7. The Alps are _mountains_ .
8. Colombia and Venezuela are _countries_ in South America.
9. Colorado and Vermont are _states_ in the United States.
10. Vienna and Oslo are two _cities_ in Europe.

Regular Plural Nouns: Pronunciation of Final *-s*, and *-es*

EXAMPLES	EXPLANATIONS
(a) books, students, groups months, desks, cats	**/S/** Final *-s* is pronounced /s/ after voiceless sounds.*
(b) beds, rooms, lives years, days, dogs	**/Z/** Final *-s* is pronounced /z/ after voiced sounds.**
(c) classes, faces exercises, sizes dishes, wishes sandwiches, watches colleges, pages	**/ɪZ/** Final *-es* is pronounced /ɪz/ after "s" sounds "z" sounds "sh" sounds "ch" sounds "ge/dge" sounds. This adds an extra syllable to the noun. *Voiceless sounds: /p/t/f/k/th/. **Voiced sounds: /b/d/g/v/m/n/l/r/ and vowels.

Make the words below plural. Then, write each word in the correct pronunciation group. Read each group aloud.

✔ book	radio	dress	house	ticket	rule
thing	horse	head	list	bus	cup
car	train	boat	church	peach	hat

/S/	/Z/	/IZ/
books	radios	dresses
tickets	rules	buses
boats	things	houses
hats	heads	horses
cups	trains	churches
lists	cars	peaches

EXERCISE 8

Look at the list of common measurements. Make the measurement on the right plural. Then read the statements aloud using the verb *equals*.

½ half
⅓ one third
¼ quarter
⅔ thirds

EXAMPLE: 98.6 degrees Fahrenheit = 37 degree _s_ Celsius.

98.6 degrees Fahrenheit equals 37 degrees Celsius.

1. one foot = 12 inch _es_
2. one pound = 16 ounce _s_
3. one minute = 60 second _s_
4. one hour = 60 minute _s_
5. one day = 24 hour _s_

6. one year = 365 day _s_
7. one quart = 2 pint _s_
8. one gallon = 4 quart _s_
9. one inch = 2 1/2 centimeter _s_
10. one kilo = 2.2 pound _s_

EXERCISE 9

Rhymes. Make the nouns in italics plural. Then, read the rhymes aloud.

1. On Education

Word _s_ , *sentence* _s_ , *exercise* _s_ , *rule* _s_ ,

Dictionar*y* _ies_ , *textbook* _s_ , *page* _s_ , *school* _s_ ,

Classroom _s_ , *teacher* _s_ , *student* _s_ , –all *jewel* _s_

Of education, these are the *tool* _s_

2. On Age

Day _s_ , *week* _s_ , *month* _s_ , *year* _s_ .

Getting old? Please, no *tear* _s_ !!!

3. On Imports

The *shoe* _S_ are Brazilian,

The *glove* _s_ are Italian,

The *chef* _S_ are from France;

from South America—the salsa dance.

The *toy* _S_ are Chinese,

The *camera* _S_ are Japanese:

Tell me, what's American, please?

FOCUS 5 ＞＞＞＞＞＞＞＞＞＞＞＞＞＞＞＞＞＞＞＞＞＞＞ **FORM**

Irregular Plural Nouns

EXAMPLES	EXPLANATIONS
(a) child children man men woman women foot feet tooth teeth mouse mice	Some nouns change spelling in the plural.
(b) a deer two deer a sheep three sheep a fish four fish	Some nouns do not change in the plural.
(c) scissors pajamas glasses shorts clothes pants	Some nouns are always plural. They have no singular form.

(handwritten above table: fish – fish)

Fill in the blanks with an irregular plural noun.

1. Big Bird is eight __feet__ tall.

2. Mickey Mouse and Minnie are famous __mice__.

3. Actresses are __women__ and actors are __men__.

4. *Bambi* is a movie about __deer__.

5. Famous __people__ in Hollywood are rich.

6. Bugs Bunny has two big front __teeth__.

7. *Sesame Street* is a television show for __children__.

8. __People__ of all ages like Disney movies.

FOCUS 6 >>>>>>>>>>>>>>>>>>>>>>>>> **FORM**

Count and Noncount Nouns

COUNT NOUNS	NONCOUNT NOUNS
Can take *a/an* or *one* in the singular. **(a)** It's a job. **(b)** My vacation is for one week.	Cannot take *a/an* or *one* in the singular. **(c)** It's work.
Can take *-s* or *-es* in the plural. **(d)** They are earrings. **(e)** They're watches.	Cannot take *-s* or *-es*. **(f)** It's jewelry.
Can take a singular or plural verb. **(g)** It is a table. **(h)** They are chairs.	Always take a singular verb. **(i)** Furniture is expensive.

Some Common Noncount Nouns

food	bread	rice	sugar	bacon
fruit	cheese	fish	salt	water
coffee	tea	milk	traffic	transportation
hair	clothing	jewelry	money	furniture
love	advice	help	crime	news
work	homework	information	luck	electricity
music	mail	luggage	garbage	pollution

EXERCISE 11

Check count or noncount for each underlined noun.

	COUNT	NONCOUNT
1.		
2.		
3.		
4.		
5.		
6.		
7.		
8.		
9.		
10.		

1. <u>Money</u> is important.

2. A <u>dollar</u> is useful.

3. Grammar <u>exercises</u> are fun.

4. <u>Homework</u> is interesting.

5. <u>Fruit</u> is healthy.

6. <u>Apples</u> are my favorite fruit.

7. Here is my <u>suitcase</u>.

8. Good <u>luggage</u> is expensive.

9. <u>Mail</u> from home is important to an international student.

10. <u>Stamps</u> are cheap.

EXERCISE 12

Work with a partner. Use the words below to ask questions about the country your partner comes from.

EXAMPLE: hamburgers/popular/in . . .?

Are hamburgers popular in Russia?

Yes, they are.

No, they aren't.

1. pizza/popular/in . . .?
2. fruit/cheap/in . . .?
3. cars/big/in . . .?
4. electricity/cheap/in . . .?
5. American music/popular/in . . .?

6. housing/expensive/in . . .?
7. families/big/in . . .?
8. taxes/high/in . . .?
9. public transportation/good/in . . .?
10. American movies/popular/in . . .?

Now make three questions on your own.

FOCUS 7 >>>>>>>>>>>>>>>>>>>> FORM/USE

How Much Is/How Much Are . . .?

EXAMPLES	EXPLANATIONS
(a) Singular: How much is a television set in China? **(b) Plural:** How much are newspapers in Russia? **(c) Noncount:** How much is gas in Italy?	To ask about prices use: **How much is . . .?** **How much are . . .?**

EXERCISE 13

Work with a partner. Ask your partner questions about prices in the country he or she is from, using *How much is/are* . . .? Your partner gives the answer in United States dollars.

EXAMPLE: jeans/in . . .?

How much are jeans in Turkey?

Answer: Jeans are about 50 dollars.

1. a bus ticket/in . . .?
2. a compact disc/in . . .?
3. bread/in . . .?
4. sneakers/in . . .?
5. a movie ticket/in . . .?

6. an apartment/in . . .?
7. bananas/in . . .?
8. a hamburger/in . . .?
9. chocolate/in . . .?
10. a local telephone call/in . . .?

loaf of bread

Be + Adjective + Noun

EXAMPLES	EXPLANATIONS
(a) Harvard and Yale are **private** universities.	An adjective can come before the noun.
(b) They are **excellent** colleges.	Do not put -s on the adjective when the noun is plural.
(c) It's **a** large university. **(d)** English is **a** universal language.	Use *a* before an adjective with a consonant or a consonant sound.
(e) He's **an** "A" student. **(f)** She's **an** honor student.	Use *an* before an adjective with a vowel sound.
(g) Psychology is a **very** interesting subject.	Put *very* before the adjective to make the adjective stronger.

EXERCISE 14

Make sentences using *be* + adjective + *very* + noun. Choose an adjective from the list. You can use an adjective more than once.

exciting	violent	tall	expensive	dangerous	
crowded	popular	talented	useful	interesting	famous

1. The Twin Towers __are very tall__ buildings in New York City.
2. Disneyworld __is a very popular__ place in Florida.
3. Luciano Pavarotti __is a very talented__ singer.
4. *Rambo* and *The Terminator* __are very exciting__ movies.
5. A Mercedes __is a very expensive__ car.
6. Teaching __is a very interesting__ profession.
7. Baseball __is a very famous__ sport in the United States and Japan.
8. Sao Paolo __is a very crowded__ city.
9. Eleanor Roosevelt and Jacqueline Kennedy Onassis __are very famous__ women in American history.
10. Computers __are very useful__ tools.

Activities

CATEGORIZING GAME.

STEP ❶ Get into two teams. Write the words in the box in the correct categories below.

STEP ❷ Then, next to each word, write C for count nouns and NC for noncount nouns.

STEP ❸ Each correct answer is one point. The team with the most points wins.

shirts	ears	coffee	shoes	feet	tea
toothpaste	underwear	lemonade	soap	coat	rice
cheese	shampoo	bread	jacket	eyes	head
hair	toothbrush	.juice	beans	milk	pizza
soda	hairbrush	hamburger	socks	towels	arm

Things to Wear   **Things to Eat**   **Things to Drink**

shirts   C
_____   _____   _____

_____   _____   _____

_____   _____   _____

_____   _____   _____

_____   _____   _____

Things in the Bathroom   **Parts of the Body**

_____   _____

_____   _____

_____   _____

_____   _____

_____   _____

ACTIVITY 2

Plan a party for the class. Get into groups. Each group plans what they are going to bring to the party under the following categories.

Food   Drink   Entertainment

Compare your plans with the other groups'. Which group has the best plan?

ACTIVITY 3

Say three or four things about a famous person. The class will guess his or her name.

EXAMPLE: She's an actress. She's French. She's blonde. She's beautiful.

Who is she?

Class guesses: Catherine Deneuve.

ACTIVITY 4

Tell your classmates what you have for:

Breakfast	Lunch	Dinner	Snack
coffee			
cereal			
orange juice			

ACTIVITY 5

STEP ❶ Listen to what kind of pizza the woman orders.

STEP ❷ Check (✔) what the woman wants on the pizza.
Then mark C for count nouns and NC for noncount nouns.

❑ cheese _____   ❑ pepperoni _____

❑ tomatoes _____   ❑ mushrooms _____

❑ olives _____   ❑ anchovies _____

❑ peppers _____   ❑ onions _____

STEP ❸ Ask a classmate about his or her favorite pizza.

STEP ❹ Role play. Telephone the pizza store with your order.

UNIT

The Verb *Have*
Affirmative and Negative Statements, Questions and Short Answers, Some/Any

OPENING TASK

Modern and Traditional Lifestyles

Look at the photographs of two Inuit women in North Canada. Check (✔) and say the things Mary has. Check and say the things Nilaulaq and her husband have.

Mary (at right)

Nilaulaq (below)

	Mary	Nilaulaq (Nila) and Her Husband, Napachee
1. a house		
2. an Inuit name		
3. Inuit clothing		
4. dogs		
5. furniture		
6. electricity		
7. fresh fish		
8. a bed		

In the photographs, who has a traditional lifestyle? Who has a modern lifestyle? Say why.

1. _____ a traditional lifestyle.

2. _____ a modern lifestyle.

Have and Has: Affirmative Statements

The verb *to have* means to own or possess.

SUBJECT	VERB	
I You	have	
He She It Mary	has	a house.
We You They (Nila & Napachee)	have	

Fill in the blanks about Nilaulaq and Mary with *have* or *has*. Read the sentences aloud.

A. Nilaulaq <u>has</u> an Inuit name. She _____ a husband. He_____ an Inuit name too. They _____ two children. They _____ two dogs. Nilaulaq says, "I _____ a beautiful family."

B. Mary _____ wallpaper in her house. Mary _____ a clock. She _____ photographs and a map. She _____ furniture. She _____ canned food.

C. Modern Inuit people live in towns. The towns _____ stores. Modern Inuit people _____ money. They _____ jobs.

Have: Negative Statements and Contractions

SUBJECT	DO/DOES	BASE FORM OF VERB	
I You We They Nilaulaq and her husband	do not (don't)	have	a telephone.
He She It Nilaulaq	does not (doesn't)		

EXERCISE 2

Make the words below into sentences with *has/have* or *doesn't have/don't have*.

Traditional families are big.

1. They/many children.

2. They also/grandmothers and grandfathers living with them.

3. In a traditional family, only the father/a job.

4. The mother/a job.

5. The children/a babysitter.

Modern families are different.

6. Sometimes they/two people.

7. Sometimes they/one or two children.

8. Sometimes, they/children.

Now make four sentences of your own about modern families.

9. _____

10. _____

11. _____

12. _____

Have: Yes/No Questions and Short Answers

DO/DOES	SUBJECT	HAVE	
Do	I you we they Nilaulaq and Napachee	**have**	a telephone?
Does	he she it Mary		

Affirmative Short Answers

Yes,	I you we they	**do.**
	he she it	**does.**

Negative Short Answers

No,	I you we they	**do not. (don't)**
	he she it	**does not. (doesn't)**

EXERCISE 3

Find Someone Who

Ask your classmates if they have the things on the left. Write the names of the students who say "yes."

EXAMPLE: Do you have a telephone?

Yes, I do. OR No, I don't.

Things	**Students' Names**
1. a cordless telephone	_____
2. pets	_____
3. a car	_____
4. children	_____
5. relatives in this country	_____
6. a job	_____
7. English-speaking friends	_____
8. a bicycle	_____
9. a driver's license	_____
10. a video cassette recorder (VCR)	_____

Work with a partner. Take turns asking and answering questions. Make questions about the Inuit people in the Task. Use short answers.

EXAMPLE: You: Does Mary have a house?

Your Partner: Yes, she does.

1. Nilaulaq/children
2. Mary/bed
3. Napachee/boat.
4. Nila/wallpaper in her house

5. Nilaulaq/furniture
6. Mary/an Inuit name
7. Nilaulaq/a television set
8. Mary/canned food

Read about the Amish people. Then work with a partner. Take turns asking and answering questions. Give short answers.

The Amish are a special group of Americans. There are about 85,000 Amish people in the United States. They have their own language. They also have a simple way of life.

The Amish are farmers, but they don't have machines on their farms. They have horses. They do not have electricity or telephones in their homes.

The Amish are called "the plain people." They wear dark clothing. The men all have beards and wear hats. The women wear long dresses and hats.

Amish children have one-room schoolhouses. They have Amish teachers. They have no school after the eighth grade.

EXAMPLE: An Amish man/car?

        You: Does an Amish man have a car?

        Your Partner: No, he doesn't.

1. Amish people/a simple life?   _____?

                                                       _____.

2. Amish women/jewelry?   _____?

                                                       _____.

3. Amish home/electricity?   _____?

                                                       _____.

4. An Amish farmer/horses?   _____?

                                                       _____.

5. An Amish home/telephone?   _____?

                                                       _____.

6. Amish people/their own language?   _____?

                                                       _____.

7. An Amish child/computer?   _____?

                                                       _____.

8. Amish people/colorful clothing?   _____?

                                                       _____.

9. An Amish home/television?   _____?

                                                       _____.

10. Amish children/special teachers?   _____?

                                                       _____.

11. Amish children/school after eighth grade? _____?

                                                       _____.

12. Amish people/a modern lifestyle?   _____?

                                                       _____.

Some/Any

EXAMPLES		EXPLANATIONS
STATEMENT	**(a)** The children have **some** books.	Use *some* in a statement.
	(b) They have **some** money.	
NEGATIVE	**(c)** They don't have **any** books.	Use *any* in a negative sentence.
	(d) She doesn't have **any** money.	
QUESTION	**(e)** Do they have **any** books?	Use *any* in a question.
	(f) Does she have **any** money?	
(g) They don't have **any** books. (plural count noun)		Use *any* with plural count nouns and noncount nouns.
(h) He doesn't have **any** money. (noncount noun)		

EXERCISE 6

Complete the rhyme with *some* or *any*.

I don't have (1) _any_ time today

I have (2) _____ problems to solve.

I have (3) _____ bills to pay

Do you have (4) _____ time to play?

I have (5) _____ places to go

I have (6) _____ people to see

Do you have (7) _____ advice for me?

Yes, I do: "Slow down!"

Fill in *some* or *any* in the sentences below. Say if the sentence is true or not true. If it is not true, change the verb and change some/any. Then say what you think . . . is it good or bad? Why?

EXAMPLE: An Amish person has __some__ friends.   True

Amish people have __some__ music.   Not true. Amish people don't have any music.

I think this is good/bad . . .

1. The Amish people don't have _____ cars.

2. Amish homes have _____ books.

3. An Amish woman has _____ jewelry.

4. An Amish woman doesn't have _____ make-up.

5. The Amish have _____ special schools.

6. Amish schools have _____ computers.

7. An Amish child doesn't have _____ school after eighth grade.

8. An Amish farmer has _____ machines.

9. Amish people have _____ colorful clothing.

10. Amish children don't have _____ American toys.

FOCUS 5 ▷▷▷▷▷▷▷▷▷▷▷▷▷▷▷▷▷▷▷▷▷▷▷ USE

Asking for Something Politely

Use *Do you have . . .?* to ask for something politely.

EXAMPLES	EXPLANATIONS

Use:
  (a) Do you have an eraser?
Answer
  (b) Yes, I do. OR Sure.
	• to ask for something politely.

Use:
  (c) Excuse me, do you have the time?
Answer
  (d) No, I don't. OR Sorry, I don't.
	• to stop a person and ask for something.

EXERCISE 8

Ask for something politely. Use *a/an/any* and the nouns below the pictures.

EXAMPLE: (pen)

Do you have a pen?

Yes, I do. OR

Sorry, no I don't.

1. (coffee)

3. (milk)

2. (match)

4. (stamps)

5. (change)

7. (sugar)

6. (eraser)

Using *Have* to Describe People

He **has** short hair.
He **has** a mustache.

HAIR COLOR	HAIR LENGTH	HAIR TYPE	OTHER	EYE COLOR
dark	long	straight	a mustache	black
light	short	wavy	a beard	brown
black	medium-length	curly	bangs	blue
brown				green
red				gray
blond				
gray				
white				

Look at the photographs of Mary and Nilaulaq and of the Amish. Fill in the blanks with *be* or *have* and the correct nouns.

1. John Lapp is Amish.

   He <u>is</u> married.

   He _____ long _____.

   He _____ a long _____.

2. Nilaulaq _____ an Inuit name.

   She _____ long black _____.

   She _____ a nice smile.

3. Daniel _____ a young Amish boy.

   He _____ long blond hair.

   He _____ bangs.

4. Mary _____ a modern Inuit woman.

   Mary _____ a round face.

   She _____ dark hair.

Correct the mistakes in the sentences.

1. He h~~ave~~ a car.   *has*

2. She have not a house.

3. He no have a TV set.

4. He doesn't is rich.

5. She doesn't has children.

6. Does he has a sister?

7. Does she is an Inuit?

8. Excuse me, have you change?

Activities

ACTIVITY 1

WHO IS HE OR SHE?

Describe one of your classmates. Do not write the person's name. Read your written description to the class. Your classmates guess who it is.

EXAMPLE: This student is tall. He has short black hair. He has brown eyes. He has a mustache. Who is he?

ACTIVITY 2

Think of a person or people you know with traditional lifestyles. Write about these people. Write about what they look like. Tell how their lives are different. Tell what they have and what they don't have. Then make an oral presentation to the class.

ACTIVITY 3

Go to the library and take out a book about the Inuit or the Amish. Write down five new things you have learned about what they have and don't have.

ACTIVITY 4

What American things do people in your country have today? Is it good or bad to have these things? Discuss this with a partner.

EXAMPLE: In my country today, we have fast-food restaurants. This is bad/good because . . .

ACTIVITY 5

 STEP ❶ Listen to this news report. Then fill in the blanks with information from the news report.

In Zorlik—*Not Any*   **On the American airplanes—*Some***

_____   _____

_____   _____

_____   _____

STEP ❷ Tell the class about a place in the world where things are bad. Use *some* and *any*.

EXAMPLE: In Zaire, many children don't have any food to eat.

UNIT

6

This/That/These/Those
Possessives

Wally the Waiter

Wally the waiter is new at his job.

STEP ❶ Ask your partner questions about the names of all the foods on Wally's tray.

STEP ❷ Read the conversation

Wally: Uh, excuse me, whose steak is this?

Charles: It's not ours.

Wally: Oh, I'm sorry. Is this your soup?

Charles: Yes, it is.

Wally: Then this bread is yours too . . . and what about these french fries?

Jim: No, the french fries aren't ours.

Wally: This salad?

Jim: That's mine.

Wally: And the pizza?

Charles: That's his pizza.

Wally: Is the hamburger for this table?

Charles: No, it isn't. But those strawberries are.

Wally: I'm very sorry. Today is my first day on this job. I'm a little confused.

Jim: No problem. But those are our sodas too, please.

Wally: Sure, thanks again for your patience!

STEP ❸ Try to help Wally remember whose foods these are. You ask questions. Your partner answers.

Foods	Charles	Jim	Someone Else
a. sodas	❑	❑	❑
b. hamburger	❑	❑	❑
c. french fries	❑	❑	❑
d. strawberries	❑	❑	❑
e. salad	❑	❑	❑
f. steak	❑	❑	❑
g. soup	❑	❑	❑
h. pizza	❑	❑	❑
i. bread	❑	❑	❑

FOCUS 1 >>>>>>>>>>>>> FORM/MEANING

This, These, That, Those

NEAR SPEAKER	FAR FROM SPEAKER
SINGULAR	
(a) **This** is a hamburger. **(b)** **This** hamburger is good.	**(c)** **That** is a steak. **(d)** **That** steak is delicious.
PLURAL	
(e) **These** are baked potatoes. **(f)** **These** baked potatoes are hot.	**(g)** **Those** are french fries. **(h)** **Those** french fries are salty.
NONCOUNT	
(i) **This** is Italian bread. **(j)** **This** Italian bread is round.	**(k)** **That** is French bread. **(l)** **That** French bread is long.

EXERCISE 1

Go back to the Opening Task on page 80. Find at least five sentences with *this*, *these*, *that*, and *those*. Write them below.

1. _____ .

2. _____ .

3. _____ .

4. _____ .

5. _____ .

EXERCISE 2

Are the things in the pictures singular, plural, or noncount? Are the things near or far from the speaker? Fill in the blanks with *this/that/these/those* and the correct form of the verb *be*.

1. <u>That</u>   <u>is</u>
   a sweater.

2. _____ _____
   high-heeled shoes.

3. _____ _____
   a belt.

4. _____ _____
   shorts.

5. _____ _____
   a dress.

6. _____ _____
   sunglasses.

7. _____ _____
   jewelry.

8. _____ _____
   a skirt.

9. _____ _____
   blouses.

10. _____ _____
    women's clothing.

Asking What Things Are

QUESTION	ANSWER
(a) What's **this**? **that**	**Singular** **It's a** sandwich. **It's an** egg.
(b) What are **these**? **those**	**Plural** **They are** french fries. **They're** cookies.
(c) What's **this** dish? **that** dish?	**Noncount** **It's** soup.

This is Maria's first American party. She doesn't know about American food. She asks her American friend, Chris, about the food on the table.

Ask questions with *what*. Then fill in the subject, verb, and *a/an* where necessary. Then match each sentence to the picture.

Letter in the Picture

1. _What's this? It's a_____ hamburger.   _d_

2. _____ hot dog.   _____

3. _____ french fries   _____

4. _____ ketchup.   _____

5. _____ pizza.   _____

6. _____ sandwich.   _____

7. _____ doughnuts.   _____

8. _____ cookies.   _____

9. _____ muffin.   _____

10. _____ ice cream.   _____

FOCUS 3 >>>>>>>>>>>>>>>>>>>>>>>> FORM

Possessive Nouns

EXAMPLES	EXPLANATIONS
(a) The boy has a dog. The **boy's dog** is small. **(b)** Carol has a magazine. **Carol's magazine** is on the table.	Add an apostrophe (') and -s to a singular noun.
(c) The boss has an office. The **boss's office** is big. The **boss' office** is big. **(d)** Charles has a sister. **Charles's** sister is twenty-six. **Charles'** sister is twenty-six.	Add an apostrophe (') and -s or just an apostrophe (')to singular nouns and names that end in -s.
(e) The waiters have trays. The **waiters' trays** are heavy.	Add only an apostrophe (') at the end of a plural noun.
(f) The **children's school** is near here. **(g)** **Women's clothing** is cheap here.	Add apostrophe (') -s to irregular plural nouns.
(h) Paul and **Mary's dog** is friendly. **(i)** My mother-in-**law's cookies** are delicious.	For two or more subjects or a subject with hyphens (-_, add '-s at the end of last noun.

EXERCISE 4

Complete these sentences about Madeline the movie star and her family. Fill in the blanks with the possessive nouns in parentheses.

1. (The movie star) _____ life is very exciting.

2. (Madeline) _____ clothes are expensive.

3. (friends) Her _____ homes are big.

4. (brother) Her _____ wife is a lawyer.

5. (husband) Her _____ name is Mark.

This/That/These/Those *Possessives*   **85**

6. (husband) Her _____ mother is very nice.

7. (parents) His _____ home is near the ocean.

8. (sister) His _____ hobby is motorcycling.

9. (children) Their _____ lives are busy.

10. (grandparents) Her _____ car is very large.

EXERCISE 5

This is Charles's family tree. Read the sentences. Write each person's relationship to Charles under the name in the box.

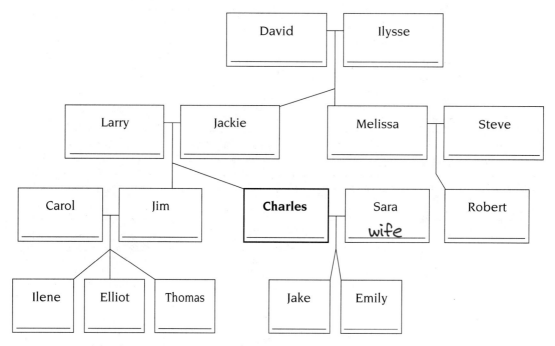

1. Sara is Charles's wife.

2. Emily is Charles's daughter.

3. Jake is Charles's son.

4. Jim is Charles's brother.

5. Carol is Charles's sister-in-law.

6. Elliot and Thomas are Charles's nephews.

7. Ilene is Charles's niece.

8. Melissa is Charles's aunt.

9. Steve is Charles's uncle.

10. Robert is Charles's cousin.

11. Jackie is Charles's mother.

12. Larry is Charles's father.

13. David is Charles's grandfather.

14. Ilysse is Charles's grandmother.

Write the correct possessive nouns in the blanks. Say each sentence aloud.

EXAMPLE: Sara is _Charles's_ wife.

1. Charles is _____ brother.

2. David is _____ father.

3. Emily is _____ sister.

4. Jim is _____ husband.

5. Melissa is _____ daughter.

6. Elliot is _____ cousin.

7. Jim is _____ uncle.

8. Jake is _____ nephew.

9. Carol is _____ sister-in-law.

10. Ilysse is _____ mother-in-law.

Look carefully at the apostrophes in the sentences below. How many people are there in each sentence? How many dogs? Check *one* or *more than one* for each sentence.

	How many people?		How many dogs?	
	One	More than one	One	More than one
1. My daughter's dog is big.	✔	_____	✔	_____
2. My daughters' dogs are big.	_____	_____	_____	_____
3. My son's dog is big.	_____	_____	_____	_____
4. My sons' dogs are big.	_____	_____	_____	_____
5. My sons' dog is big.	_____	_____	_____	_____
6. My son's dogs are big.	_____	_____	_____	_____
7. My children's dog is big.	_____	_____	_____	_____
8. My children's dogs are big.	_____	_____	_____	_____

Possessive Adjectives, Pronouns

POSSESSIVE ADJECTIVES		POSSESSIVE PRONOUNS	
My	car is new.	The car is	**mine.**
Your	house is beautiful.	The house is	**yours.**
His	dog is old.	The dog is	**his.**
Its	fur is white.	(*Its* cannot be a possessive pronoun.)	
Her	jewelry is expensive.	The jewelry is	**hers.**
Our	children are cute.	The children are	**ours.**
Their	television is big.	The television is	**theirs.**

NOTE: Do not confuse a possessive adjective (*its*) with the contraction of *it* + *is* (*it's*).

Use possessive determiners with parts of the body.

My hair is black..

Your eyes are blue.

EXERCISE 8

Describe a person in the class to your partner without saying his or her name. Your partner guesses who he or she is.

EXAMPLE: You say: Her hair is black. Her eyes are blue. Her skin is dark.

Your partner says: Is it Luisa?

EXERCISE 9

Fill in each blank with a possessive word (a possessive adjective or a possessive pronoun). Then look at the two dogs. Whose dog is A? Whose dog is B?

Many people have pets. (1) __Their_____ pets are very important to them.

Charles's family loves pets. (2) _____ children have a dog. Emily says the

dog is (3) _____, Jake says the dog is (4) _____.

(5) _____ dog is small. (6) _____ legs are short,

(7) _____ ears are long. It's cute.

Charles's parents have a dog too. They introduce their dog: "This is
(8) _____ dog. (9) _____ name is Buck. He's strong.
(10) _____ nose is flat. (11) _____ fur is short. We love
Buck. He's part of (12) _____ family."

A. It's _____ dog.

B. It's _____ dog.

Questions with W*hose*

Use *whose* to ask who owns or possesses something.

WHOSE	NOUN	VERB		ANSWERS
Whose	dog	is	this?	It's Carol's dog. It's her dog. It's hers. Carol's.
Whose	glasses	are	these?	They're Jim's glasses. They're his glasses. They're his. Jim's.

Who's and Whose

EXAMPLES	EXPLANATIONS
(a) **Who's** she? My sister. (b) **Whose** car is that? Mine.	Do not confuse *who's* and *whose*. *Who's* and *whose* have the same pronunciation. *Who's* = *who is*. *Whose* asks about who owns something.

EXERCISE 10

Ask questions with *whose* to find out who owns each object. Answer in two ways as in the example.

EXAMPLE: Whose hammer is it?

It's Jackie's hammer. It's hers.

A. John is a hairdresser. B. Jackie is a . carpenter C. Jim is a . secretary D. Pierre and Daniel are cooks.

1. spoon

2. pencil sharpener

3. shampoo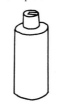

4. screwdriver

5. computer

6. comb

7. hammer

8. hairbrush

9. sauce pan

10. scissors

11. envelope

12. can opener

13. ladder

14. nails

15. frying pan

16. paperclip

EXERCISE 11

Correct the mistakes in the following sentences.

1. This is Jim magazine
2. Charles is married. Sara is her wife.
3. That computer is her's.
4. Is Jim the brother of Charles?
5. Who's son-in-law is Charles?
6. Charles and Sara have two children. Jake and Emily are theirs children.
7. What's that name's man?
8. The Larry's dog is small.
9. Whose hungry?
10. This dogs are cute.
11. A: Is this the dog's food?
    B: Yes, that's its.
12. The teacher has chalk on the face.

Activities

ACTIVITY 1

STEP ❶ Draw your family tree.

STEP ❷ Ask a classmate about his or her family tree. Draw your classmate's family tree. Then write five sentences about your classmate's family.

ACTIVITY 2

The teacher asks each student to put a personal object into a bag. One student picks an object and asks, "Whose is this?" The class guesses who the owner is. If the class is not correct, the owner says, "It's mine."

ACTIVITY 3

STEP ❶ Bring something to class that is special from your country or another country you know (something you eat, something you wear, something people use, etc.). Tell the class about the special thing.

> **EXAMPLE:** This is a special dress. It's for a wedding.

STEP ❷ Choose one of the objects from the class. Write about it.

ACTIVITY 4

Bring in a menu from an American restaurant. Ask questions about the foods on the menu. Role-play a dialogue between a confused waiter (like Wally) and two customers in a restaurant.

ACTIVITY 5

STEP ❶ Listen to the conversation. What are the people talking about?

STEP ❷ Listen again. In the chart, write *this/that/these* or *those* next to each thing. Then check (√) if each thing is *near* or *far from* the speaker.

This/that/these/those?		Near	Far from
1. these	chairs	√	
2.	table		
3.	lamp		
4.	pictures		
5.	statue		
6.	sofa		

UNIT

7

There Is/There Are
A/An versus The

OPENING TASK

Whose Apartment Is This?

Read the statements on the next page. Then circle the type of person you think lives in this apartment. Give reasons for your choice.

1. The person   is   a man/a woman.
2. The person   has   a baby/doesn't have a baby.
3. The person   has   a pet/doesn't have a pet.
4. The person   is   athletic/not athletic.
5. The person   drinks   coffee/doesn't drink coffee.
6. The person   is   well-educated/not well-educated.
7. The person   loves   music/doesn't love music.
8. The person   is   on a diet/not on a diet.

What are your reasons?

FOCUS 1 >>>>>>>>>>>>>>>>> MEANING/USE

There + Be

EXAMPLES	EXPLANATIONS
	Use *there + be*:
(a) There are a lot of things in the apartment.	• to show something or somebody exists.
(b) There is a cat under the bed.	• to show something or somebody's location.
(c) There is a mouse in the house. NOT: A mouse is in the house.	• when you talk about something or somebody for the first time.
(d) There are two men in the picture. **They are** not happy.	Do not confuse *there are* and *they are*.

EXERCISE 1

Circle (a) or (b) for the correct sentence.

EXAMPLE: (a)   Two men are in this picture.

(b)   There are two men in this picture.

1. An angry restaurant customer says,

   (a) "Waiter, a fly is in my soup."

   (b) "Waiter, there's a fly in my soup."

2. The waiter answers,

   (a) "Sorry, sir. There's more soup in the kitchen."

   (b) "Sorry, sir. More soup is in the kitchen."

3. The customer gets the bill. He says,

   (a) "Waiter, a mistake is on the bill."

   (b) "Waiter, there's a mistake on the bill."

 FOCUS 2 >>>>>>>>>>>>>>>>>>>>>> **FORM**

There Is/There Are

The form of the *be* verb depends on the noun phrase that follows it.

THERE + BE	NOUN PHRASE		EXPLANATIONS
(a) There is	an angry man	at the table.	singular count noun
(b) There are	two people	in the restaurant.	plural count noun
(c) There is	soup	in his dish.	noncount noun
(d) There is	a dining room, kitchen, and restroom	in this restaurant.	When there is more than one noun, *be* agrees with the first noun.

Contractions: *There is* = *There's*.

EXERCISE 2

Go back to the Opening Task on page 93. Write sentences about the picture with *there is/are* and the words below.

EXAMPLE: one bed in the apartment

> *There's one bed in the apartment.*

1. a tennis racquet in the closet

2. high-heeled shoes in the closet

3. women's clothing in the closet

4. sneakers in the closet

5. a coat in the closet

6. CDs on the shelf

7. a CD player on the shelf

8. books on the shelf

9. women's jewelry in the box on the table

10. coffee in the coffee pot

11. a big cake on the counter

12. an exercise bicycle in the apartment

13. an expensive rug on the floor

14. two pillows on the bed

EXERCISE 3

STEP ❶ Get into groups. Choose one student to read the following sentences. Listen to the description and draw the picture.

STEP ❷ Compare your drawings.

1. There's a table in the center of the room.

2. There are two chairs at the table—one at each end.

3. There's a tablecloth on the table.

4. There's a plate on each end of the table. On one plate, there's a steak and potatoes.

5. The other plate is empty. There's only a napkin.

6. Next to the empty plate, there's an empty glass.

7. Next to the plate with food, there's a half-full glass.

8. There's a bottle of water on the right side of the table. The bottle is half full.

9. There is a vase in the center of the table.

10. There are eight flowers on the floor next to the table.

STEP ❸ Choose the best title for your picture.

A. A Wonderful Dinner

B. Disappointed Again!

C. Always Eat Your Vegetables

There Isn't/There Aren't/
There's No/There Are No

THERE	BE		TYPE OF NOUN
There	isn't	a vase on the table.	singular count noun
There	aren't	any children in this restaurant.	plural count noun
There	isn't	any water on the table.	noncount noun

THERE	BE	NO	
There	is		vase on the table
There	are	no	children in the restaurant.
There	's		water on the table.

EXERCISE 4

Go back to the Opening Task on page 93. Make sentences with *there is/are, there isn't/there aren't*, or *there's no/there are no* with the words below.

EXAMPLE: There isn't an armchair in the apartment.

OR There's no armchair in the apartment.

1. television set
2. rug
3. men's clothing
4. computer
5. window
6. desk
7. books
8. toys
9. exercise bicycle
10. plants
11. coffee pot
12. ties

EXERCISE 5

Use the information in the chart on the next page about the city Utopia. Write sentences with *there is/are, there isn't/there aren't*, or *there's no/there are no*.

EXAMPLE: In Utopia, there aren't any guns.

In Utopia, there are no guns.

THE CITY OF UTOPIA

	Yes	No		Yes	No
1. guns		X	6. universities	X	
2. public transportation	X		7. noise		X
3. crime		X	8. jobs	X	
4. museums	X		9. parks	X	
5. traffic problems		X	10. poor people		X

EXERCISE 6

Read the politician's speech about the city of Utopia. Fill in the blanks with *there is/are*, *there isn't/there aren't*, or *there's no/there are no*.

Good evening, Ladies and Gentlemen. I am the Mayor of Utopia. I am here tonight to talk about our wonderful city.

Today, (1) __there are__ 50,000 people in our city. We are all happy. (2) _____ problems in our city.

(3) _____ jobs for all our people. (4) _____ good schools for the children. (5) _____ nice houses for all our families. The houses are comfortable. They aren't expensive.

(6) _____ homeless people on our streets. Our streets are safe. (7) _____ crime here. (8) _____ drugs. Our streets are clean. (9) _____ garbage on the streets. (10) _____ pollution.

(11) _____ many museums, theaters, and parks in our city. (12) _____ entertainment for everyone. (13) _____ good and cheap public transportation for everyone.

(14) _____ many reasons why Utopia is a great city! (15) _____ a good quality of life here in Utopia. And don't forget: (16) _____ an election this year. I want to be your Mayor for four more years. Are you happy in Utopia? Then (17) _____ only one thing to do: VOTE FOR ME, your Mayor Lucas Lime, on November sixth!

Yes/No Questions with *There Is/There Are*

YES/NO QUESTIONS	SHORT ANSWERS	TYPE OF NOUN
(a) Is there a computer in the room?	Yes, there is. No, there isn't.	singular count noun
(b) Are there any books on the shelves?	Yes, there are. No, there aren't.	plural count noun
(c) Is there any jewelry in the box?	Yes, there is. No there isn't.	noncount noun

---

EXERCISE 7

Complete the questions for each picture.

1. __Are there_____ any messages for me?

3. _____ any food in here, Mom?

2. _____ a doctor in the house?

4. _____ a post office near here?

5. _____ any tickets available for the 10:00 show?

8. _____ any mail for me?

6. _____ any room for me?

9. _____ any small sizes?

7. _____ any instructions in the box?

10. _____ a seat for me?

Test your knowledge. Ask your partner *yes/no* questions with Is *there/Are there* and the words below.

EXAMPLE: eggs in an eggplant?

Are there any eggs in an eggplant?

No, there aren't.

1. rain in a desert
2. two billion people in China
3. fifty-two states in the United States
4. earthquakes in Japan

5. billions of stars in the sky
6. life on the moon
7. trees at the North Pole
8. cure for the common cold

FOCUS 5 >>>>>>>>>>>>>>>>>>>>>>> USE

Choosing A/An or *The*

A/An and *the* are articles. A/An are indefinite articles (see Unit 4). *The* is the definite article.

A/AN	THE
Use only with singular count nouns. **(a)** Susan has **a** bicycle.	Use with all nouns. **(b)** **The** bicycle is new. (singular) **(c)** **The** books are on the shelf. (plural) **(d)** **The** jewelry is in the box. (noncount)
Use to talk about a person or thing for the first time. **(e)** Susan has **a** necklace.	Use the second time you talk about a person or thing. **(f)** Susan has a necklace. **The** necklace is beautiful.
Use to classify people, animals, and things. **(g)** She is **a** businesswoman. It's **a** restaurant.	Use when both speakers know which noun they are talking about. **(h)** When's **the** party? It's at 8:00.
	Use when the noun is the only one. **(i)** **The** sun is hot.

Look at the pictures. Fill in the blanks with *a/an* or *the*.

1. **Nurse:** It's (a) _____ girl!
Congratulations, Mr. Spade.

2. **Passenger:** Boy, it's hot. Do you have
(a) _____ air conditioner in this car?

   Driver: Yes, but (b) _____ air conditioner doesn't work. Sorry about that!

3. **Husband:** What's in (a) _____ box?

   Wife: I have (b) _____ surprise for you.

   Husband: What's (c) _____ surprise?

   Wife: Open it!

4. **Man:** Do you have (a) _____ room for
tonight?

   Clerk: Sorry, sir. (b) _____ motel is full
tonight.

5. **Husband:** Do you have (a) _____ key or do I?

   Wife: I think (b) _____ key's in the car.

6. **Receptionist:** Take your feet off (a) _____ table, please young man!

7. **Woman:** Who is it?

   Mailman: It's (a) _____ mailman, Ms. Wallace. Here's your mail.

   Woman: Thanks, Mr. Brown. Have a good day!

EXERCISE 10

Read the paragraph. Fill in *a/an* or *the*. Then answer the question: *Who is Susan's brother-in-law?* (Refer to Unit 6.)

Susan owns (1) _____ restaurant. (2) _____ restaurant is very small. It has (3) _____ cook, (4) _____ cashier, and (5) _____ waiter. Susan is (6) _____ boss. Susan has (7) _____ excellent cook in (8) _____ kitchen: her mother! Susan has (9) _____ sister. Her sister is (10) _____ cashier in

(11) _____ restaurant. Her sister's husband is (12) _____ waiter. Susan's sister is (13) _____ good cashier, but her brother-in-law is not (14) _____ very good waiter. He doesn't have (15) _____ good memory and is always confused. This is (16) _____ big problem for Susan.

EXERCISE 11

Correct the mistakes in the following sentences.

1. It's a picture on a wall.
2. There are a bathroom, a kitchen, and a living room in my house.
3. There have three bedrooms and two bathrooms in the apartment.
4. Is a good restaurant in my neighborhood.
5. There aren't milk in the refrigerator.
6. In my picture, have one woman and two men.
7. Are homeless people in your city?
8. Is there a jewelry in Susan's apartment?
9. Susan owns a restaurant.
   Really? Where is a restaurant?
10. Are there any museums in your town?
    Yes, they are.
11. Excuse me, is there the men's room in this restaurant?
12. Do you have any children?
    Yes, I have the daughter.
13. Are there pollution in your city?
14. There no are women in the restaurant.
15. There are no any poor people in Utopia.

Activities

FIND THE DIFFERENCES

Work with a partner or a group. Look at the two pictures. What is different in Picture B? Write as many sentences as you can with *There is/isn't*, or *There are/aren't* in ten minutes. The person with the most correct sentences wins.

EXAMPLE: In Picture B, there is a cat.

Picture A

Picture B

ACTIVITY 2

Find out about your partner's neighborhood.

STEP ❶ Ask questions with Is *there . . .*? Are *there . . .*? Check Yes or No in the Chart.

EXAMPLE: A: Is there a hospital in your neighborhood?

B: Yes, there is. No, there isn't.

	Yes	No
supermarkets		
movie theaters		
bookstore		
hospital		
bank		
fast-food restaurants		
gas station		
post office		
public library		
schools		
crime		
coffee shop		
trees		
public transportation		

STEP ❷ Tell the class or group about your classmate's neighborhood.

ACTIVITY 3

STEP ❶ Use the categories below to find out about your classmates. Fill in the blanks with numbers of students.

Total number of classmates _____

Sex: Male _____   Female _____

Physical Characteristics: Dark eyes _____   Blue/Green eyes _____

Women with short hair _____   Women with long hair _____

Nationalities: _____

Personalities: Shy _____   Outgoing _____

Marital Status: Married _____   Single _____

Add your own categories.

STEP ❷ Write sentences about your classmates.

EXAMPLE: There are ten Mexicans, two Chinese, three Koreans, one Vietnamese, and one Brazilian in my class.

ACTIVITY 4

Think of a place that's important to you, write a short description of this place.

ACTIVITY 5

Write a letter to the mayor of your city. Write about the problems in your city or neighborhood.

EXAMPLE: Dear Mayor,

I live in _____. There are many problems in my neighborhood. . . .

ACTIVITY 6

STEP ❶ Listen to Tom's description of his neighborhood and write in the places on the map.

STEP ❷ Work with a partner. Ask about these places in Tom's neighborhood:

1. police station
2. supermarket
3. banks
4. gas station
5. laundromat
6. mini-market
7. library
8. schools

EXAMPLE: Is there a police station?

No, there isn't.

UNIT

Simple Present Tense
*Affirmative and Negative
Statements, Time Expressions:*
In/On/At, Like/Need/Want

OPENING TASK

Looking at Healthy and Unhealthy Habits

STEP ❶ Read about Fran Tick and Janice Lowe.

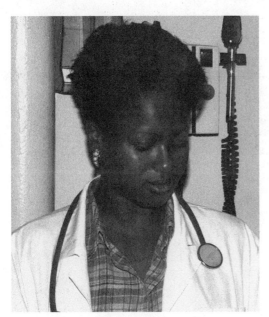

Fran Tick and Janice Lowe are friends and roommates. Fran is a doctor. She takes care of people, and she loves her job. She starts work at 6:30 A.M. and finishes at 7:30 P.M. She visits her patients in the hospital every morning. Then she hurries to her office to see other patients. She often skips meals, but she eats fruit during the day.

Janice is an accountant. She works in an office from nine to five. She's not very busy, so she often eats snacks like potato chips, cake and candy at work. After work, she plays tennis. Then she goes home and prepares a light dinner.

Fran comes home at 8:00 and eats dinner with Janice. They talk, listen to music together and relax. Then Fran goes to the gym. Janice watches television. Before bed, Janice and Fran feel hungry. They enjoy some ice cream or milk and cookies. They go to sleep at midnight.

STEP ❷ Complete the chart about Fran and Janice's healthy and unhealthy habits.

	Healthy	Unhealthy
Fran	She loves her job	She starts work at 6:30 a.m. and finishes at 7:30 p.m.
Janice		
Fran and Janice		

STEP ❸ Who is healthier? Whose life is more stressful? Why?

FOCUS 1 >>>>>>>>>>>>>>>>>>>>>>>>>> USE

Talking about Habits and Routines

EXAMPLES	EXPLANATION
(a) Fran and Janice **listen** to music together. **(b)** Fran **goes** to the gym every evening.	Use the simple present tense to talk about habits or things that happen again and again.

EXERCISE 1

Go back to the Opening Task. Underline all the simple present tense verbs that tell about Fran and Janice's habits and routines.

EXAMPLE: They <u>live</u> together.

FOCUS 2 >>>>>>>>>>>>>>>>>>>>>>>>> FORM

Simple Present Tense: Affirmative Statements

SUBJECT	VERB
I You* We They	work.
He She It	work**s**.

*Both singular and plural.

Circle the correct form of the verb.

1. Fran is a doctor. She (take/takes) care of sick people.

2. Janice is an accountant. She (work/works) in an office.

3. Fran (love/loves) her job.

4. Fran (start/starts) work at 6:30 A.M.

5. Janice (eat/eats) snacks like potato chips, cake, and candy at work.

6. Janice (prepare/prepares) a light dinner every night.

7. Fran and Janice (exercise/exercises) every day.

8. Janice (play/plays) tennis after work.

9. Fran (go/goes) to the gym.

10. They (relax/relaxes) together after dinner.

11. They (enjoy/enjoys) ice cream or milk and cookies.

12. They (go/goes) to sleep late.

Match the occupations with what they do.

1. A doctor
2. Construction workers
3. A mechanic
4. Air traffic controllers
5. A receptionist
6. Taxi drivers
7. Police officers
8. A fire fighter

a. repairs cars
b. protect people
c. answers the telephone
d. takes care of sick people
e. build houses
f. direct airplanes
g. works in emergencies
h. take passengers to different places

Which of these jobs are the most stressful? Explain why.

Third Person Singular: Spelling and Pronunciation

BASE FORM OF VERB	SPELLING	PRONUNCIATION
1. The final sound of the verb is "voiceless" (for example: p/t/f/k/s/th): **sleep**	Add -s. He **sleeps** eight hours every night.	/s/
2. The final sound of the verb is "voiced" (for example: b/d/v/g/l/m/n/r or a vowel): **prepare**	Add -s. He **prepares** dinner.	/z/
3. The verb ends in **sh, ch, x, z,** or **ss:** **watch**	Add -es. He **watches** TV.	/ɪz/
4. The verb ends in a consonant + **y:** **hurry**	Change *y* to *i* and add -es. She **hurries** home.	/z/
5. The verb ends in a vowel + **y:** **play**	Add -s. He **plays** tennis on Saturday.	/z/
6. Irregular Forms: **have** **go** **do**	Jane **has** a job. She **goes** to work every day. Fred **does** the dishes.	/z/

The pictures of Lazy Louie and his wife Hannah are not in the correct order. Number the pictures in the correct order. Then write the number of the picture next to the sentences below.

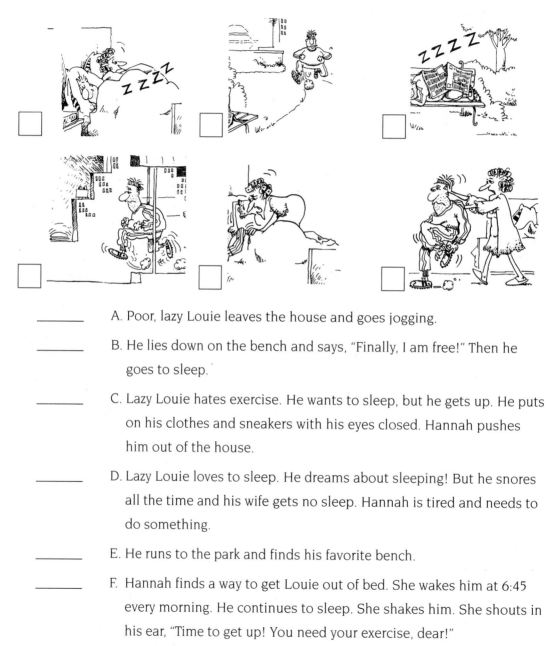

_____ A. Poor, lazy Louie leaves the house and goes jogging.

_____ B. He lies down on the bench and says, "Finally, I am free!" Then he goes to sleep.

_____ C. Lazy Louie hates exercise. He wants to sleep, but he gets up. He puts on his clothes and sneakers with his eyes closed. Hannah pushes him out of the house.

_____ D. Lazy Louie loves to sleep. He dreams about sleeping! But he snores all the time and his wife gets no sleep. Hannah is tired and needs to do something.

_____ E. He runs to the park and finds his favorite bench.

_____ F. Hannah finds a way to get Louie out of bed. She wakes him at 6:45 every morning. He continues to sleep. She shakes him. She shouts in his ear, "Time to get up! You need your exercise, dear!"

EXERCISE 5

Here is a list of third-person singular verbs from the story about Lazy Louie. Check the sound you hear at the end of the verb. Then read the verbs aloud.

Verb	/S/	/Z/	/IZ/
1. loves			
2. wakes			
3. pushes			
4. leaves			
5. lies			
6. hates			
7. puts			
8. dreams			
9. snores			
10. needs			
11. goes			
12. finds			
13. says			
14. continues			
15. shakes			
16. shouts			
17. gets			
18. wants			
19. runs			

EXERCISE 6

Sit in a circle. The first person in the circle starts to tell the story of Louie and Hannah and the next continues, and so on all around the circle.

FOCUS 4 >>>>>>>>>>>>>>>>>>>>>> **MEANING**

Frequency and Time Expressions

EXAMPLES	EXPLANATIONS
every morning/afternoon/evening/night every day/week/year every summer/winter/spring/fall all the time once a week twice a month three times a year	Frequency expressions tell how often we do something.
in + the morning 　　　the afternoon 　　　the evening in + June 　　　1939 　　　the summer at + 7:30 　　　night 　　　noon on + Wednesday(s) 　　　March 17 　　　the weekend	Time expressions tell when we do something.

EXERCISE 7

Fill in the blanks with a frequency or time expression.

Fred and Jane get up (1) _____ seven (2) _____ day of

the week, but not (3) _____ weekends. (4) _____ Satur-

day, they get up (5) _____ nine and play tennis (6) _____

the morning. (7) _____ the afternoon, they go shopping.

(8) _____ the evening, they go out with friends. They go to bed

116 　　Unit 8

(9) _____ midnight. (10) _____ Sunday, they get up

(11) _____ ten and have breakfast (12) _____ noon. They

stay home and read (13) _____ Sunday.

Frequency and Time Expressions

EXAMPLES	EXPLANATIONS
(a) They cook dinner **every night.** **(b)** She gets up at 7:00 **every morning.**	Frequency and time expressions usually come at the end of a sentence.
(c) They cook dinner **every night at 7:00.** **(d)** They cook dinner **at seven every night.**	When there is both a frequency and a time expression in one sentence, the frequency expression can come before or after the time expression.
(e) **Once a week,** they go out to eat. **(f)** **On weekends,** they stay in.	Frequency and time expressions can sometimes come at the beginning of a sentence. Use a comma (,) after the expressions at the beginning of a sentence.
(g) I work **on Saturdays.** **(h)** I work **Saturdays.**	With days and dates, *on* is not necessary.

EXERCISE 8

Make true statements about yourself using the time and frequency expressions below and the simple present tense.

EXAMPLE: once a week

> **You say:** I go to the library once a week.

1. once a week
2. every weekend
3. twice a week
4. on my birthday

5. once a year

6. at 7:30 in the morning

7. on Friday nights

8. in August

9. in the summer

10. all the time

11. on December 31

12. at 6:00

EXERCISE 9

Look at Wendy's weekly schedule. Then fill in the blanks in the exercise with the simple present tense or a frequency or time expression.

	Monday	Tuesday	Wednesday	Thursday	Friday
7:00	wake up				
7:30	eat breakfast at home				go out for breakfast
9:30	teach French	go jogging	teach French	do aerobics	teach French
12:00	eat lunch at school	eat lunch at home	eat lunch at school	eat lunch at home	attend meetings
3:00	play tennis	prepare lessons	play tennis	go food shopping	clean apartment
6:00	meet a friend for dinner	go to cooking class	go to the movies	take dancing lessons	go out with friends
8:00	do the laundry	talk on the phone	read a novel	prepare lessons	
10:30	go to bed early				
12:00					go to bed

1. Wendy _goes food shopping_ on Thursday afternoon.

2. Wendy cleans her apartment _on Friday afternoon_.

3. Wendy_____ every day at 7:00.

4. She eats breakfast at home _____.

5. Once a week, on Friday mornings, she _____.

6. She_____ three times a week.

7. She does aerobics _____.

8. She eats lunch at school _____.

9. She attends meetings _____.

10. _____ she eats lunch at home.

11. She goes to cooking class _____.

12. She reads _____.

13. On Friday evening, she _____.

14. She goes to bed early _____.

15. She _____ at midnight on Friday.

16. She does the laundry _____.

17. She _____ at 8:00 on Thursday night.

Now make two more statements about Wendy's schedule.

18. _____.

19. _____.

FOCUS 6 ⟩⟩⟩⟩⟩⟩⟩⟩⟩⟩⟩⟩⟩⟩⟩⟩⟩⟩⟩⟩⟩⟩⟩⟩ FORM

Simple Present: Negative Statements

SUBJECT	DO/DOES NOT	BASE FORM OF VERB
I You* We They Jim and Peter	do not don't	work.
He She It Mary	does not doesn't	

*Both singular and plural.

Do you have a healthy life? Check (✔)Yes or No.

	Yes	No
1. I smoke.	_____	_____
2. I exercise every day.	_____	_____
3. I drink six or more cans of soda every day.	_____	_____
4. I eat fruit and vegetables.	_____	_____
5. I eat fast food every day.	_____	_____
6. I live a quiet life.	_____	_____
7. I go to bed late.	_____	_____
8. I skip meals.	_____	_____
9. I feel tired every day.	_____	_____
10. I eat red meat every day.	_____	_____
11. I cook fresh food at home.	_____	_____
12. I find time to relax.	_____	_____
13. I overeat.	_____	_____
14. I worry all the time.	_____	_____

Now look at your partner's Yes and No checks. Does he or she have a healthy life? Tell the class why your partner has a healthy or unhealthy life.

EXAMPLE: My partner has a very healthy life. He doesn't smoke. He exercises every day.

FOCUS 7 >>>>>>>>>>>>>>>>>>>>>>>>>>> **USE**

Talking about Things that Are Always True

EXAMPLES	EXPLANATION
(a) The sun **rises** in the East. **(b)** A healthy person **enjoys** life. **(c)** A healthy person **doesn't use** drugs.	Use the simple present to make statements about things that always happen or things that are always true.

Use the simple present affirmative or negative to complete the definitions of the new words below.

1. Workaholics (love) __love_____ to work all the time.

2. Vegetarians (eat) _____ meat.

3. Couch potatoes (sit) _____ in front of the TV all the time.

4. An alcoholic (drink) _____ a lot of wine, beer, or liquor every day.

5. A pacifist (like) _____ war.

6. An insomniac (sleep) _____ at night.

7. A stressed person (worry) _____ a lot.

8. A health-conscious person (care) _____ about his or her health.

9. Environmentalists (like) _____ pollution.

Fill in the blanks. Use the simple present affirmative or negative of the verbs in parentheses.

Today, many Americans are under stress. They (move) (1) __move_____ at a

fast pace. They (work) (2) _____ all the time. They often (work)

(3) _____ overtime. An average worker (have) (4) _____

too much work and (have) (5) _____ enough time to finish it. Many

Americans (take) (6) _____ vacations. Time is important, but people

(have) (7) _____ time for themselves or their families.

Why are Americans so busy all the time? One reason is modern technology. Modern

technology (keep) (8) _____ us busy and (give) (9) _____

us stress. Technology (help) (10) _____ us relax. We (wear)

(11) _____ beepers. We (use) (12) _____ fax machines to

send messages fast. We (take) (13) _____ time to rest. Even on Sundays,

many stores (stay) (14) _____ open and people (go shopping)

(15) _____. Today, stress is one of the top reasons why Americans (get)

(16) _____ sick.

FOCUS 8 >>>>>>>>>>>>> **FORM/MEANING**

Like, Want, Need

EXAMPLES	EXPLANATIONS
I { like / want / need } coffee.	Subject + Verb + Noun
I { like / want / need } to drink coffee.	Subject + Verb + Infinitive
(a) I love animals. I **want** a cat. **(b)** I love Bill. I **want** to marry him.	*Want* expresses desire.
(c) I have a headache. I **need** some medicine. **(d)** You don't look well. You **need** to see a doctor.	*Need* expresses something that is necessary.

What do these people need? Write one sentence with *need* + noun and another sentence with *want* + infinitive. Use the nouns and verbs in the box.

EXAMPLE:

He needs some flour

He wants to bake some cookies

Nouns	Verbs
cup of coffee	write down a message
hammer	hang a picture
a quarter	fix a broken cup
peace and quiet	paint a room
pen	wake up
glue	go to sleep
a can of paint	make a telephone call

1.

_____

_____

2.

_____

_____

3.

_____
_____

4.

_____
_____

5.

_____
_____

6.

_____
_____

7.

_____
_____

Correct the mistakes in the following sentences.

1. She is smile every day.
2. He every day takes a walk.
3. He finish his dinner every night.
4. He don't cook dinner on Sundays.
5. We are study in the library on Saturdays.
6. She don't work on Tuesdays.
7. English classes begin at September.
8. She need a pen to write
9. He want to make a sandwich
10. Wendy plays tennis on 3:00.

Activities

ACTIVITY 1

Who is a person you admire? Tell your partner about him or her. Then answer questions your partner may have.

EXAMPLE: I admire my mother. She loves our family. She enjoys her work. She cooks great food. She doesn't get angry.

Who is a person you are worried about? Tell your partner about him or her. Then answer the questions your partner may have.

EXAMPLE: I am worried about my friend. He doesn't eat healthy food. He doesn't exercise. He doesn't sleep. He sits in front of the TV all the time.

With your partner choose one person you admire or are worried about. Tell the class about the person.

ACTIVITY 2

What do you and your partner have in common? Write two affirmative statements and two negative statements with *like* for each of the categories below. Share your sentences with your partner and find out what you both have in common. Report your results to the class.

Music	Books	Food
I like to listen to classical music. I also like rock. I don't like rap. I don't like to listen to opera.		
Movies	**Sports**	**Cars**

Fill out your own daily schedule using only the base form of the verb. Then exchange schedules with a partner. Write ten affirmative and negative sentences about your partner's habits and routines. Report to the class.

EXAMPLE: My partner goes jogging on Mondays at 6:00 A.M.

	Mon.	Tues.	Wed.	Thurs.	Fri.	Sat.	Sun.
Morning		6:00 go jogging					
Afternoon				3:00 go to the library			
Evening							

Write ten statements about the habits of people in the country you come from. Share your information with your classmates. Compare the habits of people in different countries.

EXAMPLES:

1. In Korea, women don't change their names when they get married.

   people eat rice every day.

   men go into the army.

2. In China, people like to exercise in the morning.

   people go to work by bicycle.

3. In Italy, people eat pasta.

ACTIVITY 5

What is a typical day for you?

Look at the activities below and say how much time you spend on each activity.

sleep _____   eat _____   work _____

study in school _____   do exercise _____   clean my room _____

watch TV _____   do homework _____   talk on the phone _____

travel _____   cook _____   get dressed _____

other _____

Get into a group and talk about each activity. What is the average time the group spends on each activity? Each group should report to the class.

EXAMPLE: We sleep eight hours a night.

Listen to the two people talk about their jobs. Complete the chart.

S = Sunday
M = Monday
T = Tuesday
W = Wednesday
T = Thursday
F = Friday
S = Saturday

Job	Start	Circle workdays	Work on Sundays?
1.		S M T W T F S	
2.		S M T W T F S	

Which job do you like? 1 or 2? Why?

UNIT

9

Simple Present Tense
Yes/No Questions, Adverbs of Frequency, Wh-Questions

OPENING TASK

What Do Good Language Learners Do?

You are all "language learners" in this class. But are you **good** language learners? What is a **good language learner**? What does a good language learner do?

STEP ❶ Read the text below. Then check Yes or No.

Good language learners think about how to learn. They try to use the new language every day. They read, write, and listen to the new language. They find people to speak to. When they don't understand, they don't get nervous. They try to guess the meanings of new words and expressions. They always ask questions about the language. They find ways to remember new words. They try to use new words and expressions in sentences. They listen to correct pronunciation. They repeat words out loud. They sometimes talk to themselves in the new language. They also think about grammar. They try to understand how the new language works.

Good language learners know that learning a new language is not easy. They don't feel bad when they make mistakes. They try to understand their problems in the new language. They review every day.

	Yes	No
1. _____ they think about how to learn?		
2. _____ they practice the new language?		
3. _____ they get nervous when they don't understand?		
4. _____ they ask questions about the new language?		
5. _____ they guess the meaning of new words?		
6. _____ they find ways to remember new words?		
7. _____ they listen to pronunciation?		
8. _____ they think about grammar?		
9. _____ they feel bad when they make mistakes?		
10. _____ they think language learning is easy?		

STEP ❷ Compare your answers with a partner's.

STEP ❸ With a partner, make up some comprehension questions about this text. For example: Do good language learners think about how to learn? Does a good language learner practice the new language?

Simple Present: *Yes/No* Questions

DO/DOES	SUBJECT	BASE FORM OF VERB	SHORT ANSWERS			
			AFFIRMATIVE		NEGATIVE	
Do	I you we they	work?	Yes,	you I we they	do.	No, you I we they do not. don't.
Does	he she it		Yes,	he she it	does.	No, he she it does not. doesn't.

EXERCISE 1

Are your classmates good language learners?

Ask one classmate *yes/no* questions with the words below. Then ask another classmate the questions.

EXAMPLE: You: Do you speak English outside of class?

      Classmate: Yes, I do./No, I don't.

	Classmate 1		Classmate 2	
	Yes	No	Yes	No
1. speak English outside of class				
2. practice pronunciation				
3. ask people to correct your English				
4. ask people questions about English				
5. watch TV in English				
6. guess the meaning of new words				

	Classmate 1		Classmate 2	
	Yes	No	Yes	No
7. make lists of new words				
8. read something in English every day				
9. write something in English every day				
10. think about grammar				

Discuss your answers with the class. Decide who is a good language learner.

EXERCISE 2

INFORMATION GAP

Nahal and Sang-Woo are two different types of language learners. Work with a partner to find out how they are different. Student A looks at the chart below. Student B looks at the chart on page E-4. Ask and answer questions to complete your chart.

EXAMPLE: **Student A:** Does Nahal want to meet English-speaking people?

Student B: Yes, she does.

Student B: Does Sang-Woo want to meet English-speaking people?

Student A: No, he doesn't.

Student A:

	Nahal		Sang-Woo	
	Yes	No	Yes	No
1. like to learn English	✔			
2. want to meet English-speaking people				✔
3. feel nervous when speaking English		✔		
4. like to work in groups			✔	
5. need grammar rules to learn English	✔			
6. learn by speaking and listening to English				✔
7. learn by reading and writing English		✔		
8. learn slowly, step by step			✔	
9. try new ways of learning	✔			

What kind of language learner are you?
Look at Exercise 2 and write statements about yourself.

EXAMPLE: _I like to learn English. I want to meet English-speaking people. I don't feel_

nervous when speaking English.

What are some of your habits? Ask a partner _yes/no_ questions with the words below. Check yes or no. Then your partner asks you.

EXAMPLE: You: Do you wake up early?

Your Partner: Yes, I do./No, I don't.

	Your Partner's Answers	
	Yes	**No**
1. wake up early	_____	_____
2. watch TV a lot	_____	_____
3. listen to loud music	_____	_____
4. cook	_____	_____
5. have parties on weekends	_____	_____
6. make friends easily	_____	_____
7. go to bed late	_____	_____
8. talk on the telephone a lot	_____	_____
9. study hard	_____	_____
10. clean your apartment every week	_____	_____

Read about students in the United States.

(1) In the United States, a child usually starts kindergarten at age five. (2) In public schools, boys and girls study together. (3) Children go to school five days a week. (4) They don't go to school on Saturdays. (5) They go to school from 8:30 A.M. to 3:00 P.M. (6) They don't wear uniforms in school. (7) In public schools, children do not study religion.

(8) In high school, every student takes difficult exams to enter college. (9) A private college costs a lot of money. (10) The government doesn't pay for private colleges. (11) Parents pay for their children's education. (12) Many students work after school to help pay for college.

Write twelve *yes/no* questions from the sentences marked 1–12 in the reading. Interview a classmate about his or her country with the questions you wrote. Compare students in the United States to students in your countries.

QUESTIONS

1. Does a child usually start kindergarten at age five in your country ?
2. Do boys and girls usually study together ?
3. _____ ?
4. _____ ?
5. _____ ?
6. _____ ?
7. _____ ?
8. _____ ?
9. _____ ?
10. _____ ?
11. _____ ?
12. _____ ?

Now write five sentences about school in your partner's country.

1. In Korea, students study religion in school.
2. _____
2. _____
3. _____
4. _____
5. _____

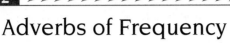

FOCUS 2 ➤➤➤➤➤➤➤➤➤➤➤➤➤➤➤➤➤➤ **MEANING**

Adverbs of Frequency

Adverbs of frequency tell how often something happens.

QUESTION: HOW OFTEN DOES NAHAL WATCH TELEVISION?

---

	always		100%
	almost always		
	usually		
Nahal	**often/frequently**	watches television.	
	sometimes		
	seldom/rarely		
	never		0%

EXERCISE 6

Read the questions and answers. Circle the correct adverbs of frequency.

EXAMPLE: Q: Does Nahal read English/American newspapers?

   A: She (⟨often⟩/seldom) reads an English or American newspaper. She buys one every morning.

1. **Q:** Does Sang-Woo ever use his hands when he speaks English?

   A: He (never/always) uses his hands. His hands help him explain things.

2. **Q:** Does Nahal ever guess the meanings of words?

   A: She (never/always) guesses the meanings of new words. She uses her dictionary all the time.

3. **Q:** Does Sang-Woo ever think in English?

   A: He (never/usually) thinks in his own language first. Then he translates his words into English.

4. **Q:** Does Nahal ever sing in English?

   A: She (often/seldom) sings in English. She doesn't like to sing.

5. **Q:** Does Sang-Woo ever write letters in English?

A: He has an American friend in Boston. He misses him. He (rarely/sometimes) writes letters to him in English.

6. **Q:** Does Nahal ever make telephone calls in English?

   A: She lives with her aunt. Her aunt speaks English. Her aunt makes the phone calls. Nahal (never/always) makes phone calls in English.

7. **Q:** Does Nahal ever talk to herself in English?

   A: She likes English. She (usually/rarely) talks to herself in English.

8. **Q:** Does Sang-Woo ever think about how English works?

   A: He thinks grammar is very interesting. He (never/always) tries to understand how English works.

EXERCISE 7

The chart below shows learning habits and adverbs of frequency. Check the box that is true for you.

Learning Habits	Adverbs of Frequency						
	ALWAYS	ALMOST ALWAYS	USUALLY	OFTEN FREQUENTLY	SOMETIMES	SELDOM RARELY	NEVER
1. use a dictionary							
2. make telephone calls in English							
3. speak to native speakers							
4. discuss learning problems with classmates							
5. practice English pronunciation							
6. record your voice on tape							
7. read books or newspapers in English							
8. ask questions about English							
9. think in English							
10. dream in English							

Position of Adverbs of Frequency

EXAMPLES	EXPLANATIONS
(a) They **always** come to class. **(b)** He **sometimes** asks questions in class. **(c)** He **never** asks questions.	Adverbs of frequency usually come between the subject and the verb.
(d) **Sometimes** I ask questions in class. **(e)** That's not true. He asks questions **often.**	Adverbs of frequency can sometimes come at the beginning or at the end of a sentence for emphasis.
(f) They **are always** in class. **(g)** I **am never** late to class.	Adverbs of frequency come after the verb *be*.

EXERCISE 8

Go back to the chart in Exercise 7. Exchange books with a partner. Write statements about your partner's learning habits using adverbs of frequency.

EXAMPLE: He always uses a dictionary.

She rarely speaks to native speakers.

EXERCISE 9

Add an adverb of frequency to make the statements below true about the country you come from.

Name of country: _____

In schools in the country I come from:

1. The students are of the same nationality.

   The students are usually of the same nationality.

2. The teachers are women.

   _____

3. Teachers hit students.

   _____

4. Teachers are young.

   _____

5. Teachers give homework.

   _____

6. Teachers are relaxed and friendly.

   _____

7. Students work together to learn.

   _____

8. The classrooms are noisy.

   _____

9. Students take tests.

   _____

10. Students cheat on tests.

   _____

Now discuss what you think is true for the United States.

FOCUS 4 >>>>>>>>>>>>>>> **FORM/MEANING**

Simple Present: W*h*-Questions

WH-QUESTION WORD	DO/DOES	SUBJECT	BASE FORM OF VERB	
(a) What	do	I	**do**	in class?
(b) When		you	**watch**	TV?
(c) What time		we	**begin**	class?
(d) Where		they	**study**	English?
(e) Why	does	he	**need**	English?
(f) How		she	**go**	to school?
(g) How often		Maria	**talk to**	native speakers of English?
(h) Who(m)		George	**meet**	after school?

EXERCISE 10

Match each question to its answer. Write the letter on the line.

f   1. Why does he need English?

_____ 2. When does the semester begin?

_____ 3. What do they do in class?

_____ 4. What time does your class start?

_____ 5. Where does he study English?

_____ 6. How often does he speak English?

_____ 7. When does she go out with her girlfriends?

_____ 8. How does he go home?

a. on weekends

b. by car

c. at the City University of New York.

d. They speak, read, write, and listen to English.

e. at 8:30

f. because he wants to go to college in the United States

g. on September 10th

h. every day

Read the story of a student named Denise. Write *Wh*-questions with the words in parentheses. Then read the text again and answer the questions aloud.

Denise is a Haitian student in New York. She speaks three languages—Creole, French, and English. She wants to be a bilingual teacher. Her English is very good, but she speaks with an accent. Sometimes people don't understand her when she speaks. She often meets her Haitian friends to talk about her problem. Denise feels embarrassed and seldom speaks English. She feels angry at Americans. She says Americans only speak English. They don't understand the problems people have when they learn a new language.

EXAMPLE: (Denise/live) <u>Where does Denise live</u> _____ ?

1. (Denise/come from) _____ ?

2. (Denise/want to be) _____ ?

3. (Denise/speak English) _____ ?

4. (Denise/feel when she speaks English) _____ ?

5. (Denise/feel this way) _____ ?

6. (Denise/feel angry) _____ ?

Now ask two questions of your own about the story.

7. _____ ?

8. _____ ?

Wh-Questions with Who/Whom

EXAMPLES	EXPLANATIONS
(a) Q: Who usually meets her friends? 　**A:** Denise. **(b) Q: Who** speaks Creole? 　**A:** Denise and her Haitian friends.	*Who* asks a question about the subject (Denise) of the sentence. Do not use *do/does*.
(c) Q: Who(m) does Denise meet? 　**A:** Denise meets her friends.	*Who(m)* asks a question about the object (her friends) of the sentence.
(d) Whom does Denise call on Sundays? **(e) Who** does Denise call on Sundays?	Formal written English Informal or spoken English
(f) Q: What goes up but never comes down? 　**A:** Your age!	*What* can also be the subject of a question. Do not use *do/does* in this case.

EXERCISE 12

Fill in the blanks with *who* or *whom*.

EXAMPLE: __Who__ speaks English?

　　　　　__Who(m)__ do you call every week?

1. _____ likes English?

2. _____ avoids English?

3. _____ bites his or her nails before a test?

4. _____ do you meet after class?

5. _____ do you usually visit on weekends?

6. _____ makes mistakes in English?

7. _____ do you call at night?

8. _____ understands the difference between *who* and *whom*?

9. _____ helps you with English?

Read about immigrant families in the United States.

Many families immigrate to the United States. At the beginning, the parents sometimes have problems. They don't speak English. They don't learn English fast. The children often learn English before the parents, so they translate for their parents. The children always help their parents. For example, the children some-times pay the rent to the landlords. They often talk with doctors about their parents' health. The children take their parents to job interviews. They solve the family's problems. This is a big job for the children, and they feel important. But their parents sometimes feel sad and helpless. Life is often difficult for new immigrant families.

Fill in the blanks with *who* (subject) or *whom* (object).

EXAMPLE: Q: _Who_ learns English before the parents?

A: The children (learn English before the parents.)

Q: _Whom_ do the children help?

A: (The children help) their parents.

1. _____ translates for the parents?

2. _____ helps the parents?

3. _____ do the children pay the rent to?

4. _____ do the children often talk to about their parents' health?

5. _____ do the children take to job interviews?

6. _____ solves the family's problems?

7. _____ feels important?

8. _____ feels sad and helpless?

Getting Information about English

In a new language, you do not always know the words to say what you want. When you have a problem, ask for help.

EXAMPLES	EXPLANATIONS
You say:	**When you:**
(a) What does the word *decision* mean?	• want to know the **meaning** of a word.
(b) What does *strategy* mean?	
(c) How do you spell *remember*?	• want to know the **spelling** of a word.
(d) How do you pronounce *communicate*?	• want to know the **pronunciation** of a word.
(e) How do you say *a machine to clean floors*?	• don't know the word for something, and you want to explain your meaning.
(f) How do you say *the opposite of happy*?	

EXERCISE 14

Ask *Wh*-questions for the answers below.

EXAMPLE: Q: How do you say special shoes you wear in the house?

　　　　　A: You say slippers.

1. **Q:** _____?

　　A: You pronounce it /ǽŋ-gwɪdʒ.

2. **Q:** _____?

　　A: The word *guess* means you don't know the answer, but you try to find the answer in your head.

3. **Q:** _____?

　　A: You say *thin*.

4. **Q:** _____?

　　A: You spell it: c-o-m-m-u-n-i-c-a-t-e.

5. **Q:** _____?

   A: *Strategy* means an action or actions you take to achieve a goal; for example. to learn English.

Correct the mistakes in the following sentences.

1. Is he read books?
2. Do they good students?
3. What means *routines*?
4. I watch sometimes TV.
5. How often you listen to native speakers of English?
6. Does he studies in the library?
7. What does the class on Mondays?
8. How you say *not correct*?
9. I am never make mistakes.
10. Why you feel embarrassed to speak English?

Activities

ACTIVITY 1

Work with a partner. Ask each other *yes/no* and *Wh*-questions in the simple present tense. Find five ways in which you are the same and five ways in which you are different. Write your questions and answers and then report to the class.

EXAMPLES: Do you eat breakfast?

What do you eat for breakfast?

ACTIVITY 2

Find the perfect roommate. You want to share an apartment with another student. Write ten questions to ask your classmates. Find a good "roommate" in your class.

EXAMPLE: • Do you smoke?   • How often do you have parties?

   • What time do you get up?   • When do you go to bed?

ACTIVITY 3

What do you know about the countries your classmates come from? Write ten questions about customs, habits, etc. Find a classmate who comes from a different country and ask the questions. Use adverbs of frequency in your questions and answers. Then report to the class.

EXAMPLES: What do people usually do on weekends?

How often do people go to the movies?

How do people usually celebrate their birthdays?

ACTIVITY 4

GENERAL KNOWLEDGE QUIZ

STEP ❶ Get into two teams. Write ten general knowledge *Wh*-questions in the simple present.

STEP ❷ Team A asks Team B the first question. Team B can discuss the question before they answer. Then Team B asks Team A the second question and so on.
Score: Score 1 point for each grammatically correct question. Score 1 point for each correct answer. The team with the most points is the winner.

EXAMPLE: Where does the President of the United States live?

When do the Chinese celebrate the New Year?

ACTIVITY 5

Write about the educational system in your native country. Answer these questions:

• What do students usually do?
• What do teachers usually do?
• What are the differences between the school system in your native country and the United States?

ACTIVITY 6

STEP ❶ Listen to the conversation between Pedro and Yuko. Who is the hard-working student?

STEP ❷ Listen again. Make a list of the things Pedro and Yuko do on Sundays.

Pedro   Yuko

_____   _____

_____   _____

_____   _____

_____   _____

STEP ❸ Role-play the conversation with a partner.

UNIT

10

Imperatives and Prepositions of Direction

OPENING TASK

Who Says What?

1.

2.

3.

4.

5.

6.

STEP ❶ Match each statement to a picture.

Picture
Number

(a) "Please give me change for a dollar, Sir." _____

(b) "Have a piece of cake with your coffee, Mary." _____

(c) "Don't ask your father now. He's very angry." _____

(d) "Don't throw your litter on the street. Pick it up!" _____

(e) "Go straight down Eighth Avenue and turn left at the bakery." _____

(f) "Watch out!" _____

STEP ❷ What is the mother saying? Write her words.

Imperatives: Affirmative and Negative

Affirmative

BASE FORM OF VERB	
(a) Have	a piece of cake.
(b) Give	me a dollar.

Negative

DON'T + BASE FORM OF VERB	
(c) Don't throw	your litter on the street.
(d) Don't ask	your father now.

Polite Imperatives

(e) Please give me change for a dollar.

(f) Please don't do that again.

(g) Don't do that again, **please.**

NOTE: Don't use a subject with imperatives:
Have a piece of cake. NOT: ~~You~~ *have a piece of cake.*

EXERCISE 1

Go back to the Opening Task on page 148. Underline all the affirmative imperatives and circle all the negative imperatives.

EXAMPLE: "Please <u>give</u> me change for a dollar, Sir."

FOCUS 2 ➤➤➤➤➤➤➤➤➤➤➤➤➤➤➤➤➤➤➤➤➤ USE

Uses of Imperatives

Imperatives have different uses or purposes. Look at the pictures and see what the imperative does in each situation.

a.

b.

c.

d.

e.

f.

150 Unit 10

IMPERATIVE	USE
(a) "Don't worry, Relax."	Give advice or make a suggestion
(b) "Be careful!"	Give a warning when there is danger.
(c) "Make a right at the corner."	Give directions or instructions.
(d) "Please give me some aspirin, Mom."	Make a polite request.
(e) "Have some coffee, dear."	Offer something politely.
(f) "Don't come home late again!"	Give an order.

EXERCISE 2

Look back at the Opening Task on page 147. Write the number of the picture that matches each use.

Use	Picture Number
A. Give advice	2
B. Give an order	
C. Give a warning when there is danger	
D. Make a polite request	
E. Offer something politely	
F. Give directions	

EXERCISE 3

Fill in each blank with an affirmative or negative imperative.

use	keep	drink	be	drive
wear	obey	leave	look	use

To be a good driver, remember these rules:

1. _____ prepared to stop.

2. _____ ahead.

3. _____ your rearview mirrors.

4. _____ the speed limit.

5. _____ space between your car and the car in front of you.

6. _____ your seat belt.

7. _____ if you are very tired or are on medication.

8. _____ and drive.

9. _____ your horn to warn others of danger.

10. _____ your car in good condition.

Work with a partner. You read each sentence on the left. Your partner gives an appropriate response from the right.

1. I don't like my landlord.	a. Go on a diet.
2. I have a headache.	b. Go to the dentist.
3. I am overweight.	c. Make friends with your classmates.
4. I have the hiccups.	d. Move to a different apartment.
5. I have a toothache.	e. Call home.
6. I don't have any friends here.	f. Go to bed early.
7. I feel tired every morning.	g. Practice speaking to native speakers.
8. I miss my family.	h. Hold your breath for two minutes.
9. I worry too much.	i. Take it easy.
10. I can't speak English very well.	j. Take some aspirin.

FOCUS 3 >>>>>>>>>>>>>>>>>>>>>>>>>> **USE**

Using Imperatives Appropriately

EXAMPLES	EXPLANATIONS
(a) Police Officer to woman: "Show me your license."	Use an imperative when: • the speaker has the right or authority to tell the listener to do something.
(b) A teacher to a teacher: "Pass me that book, please."	• the speaker and the listener are equals; for example, they work together.

Check Yes if the imperative is appropriate in each situation. Check (✔)No if the imperative is not appropriate.

Situation	Imperative	Yes	No
1. A student says to a teacher:	"Give me my paper."		
2. A student says to a classmate:	"Wait for me after class."		
3. A man stops you on the street. He says:	"Hey, mister. Tell me the time."		
4. A worker says to his boss:	"Don't bother me now. I'm busy."		
5. You get into a taxi and say:	"Take me to the airport, and please hurry!"		
6. Father says to a teenage son:	"Turn down that music! I can't take it anymore!"		

FOCUS 4 ➤➤➤➤➤➤➤➤➤➤➤➤➤➤➤➤➤➤➤ **MEANING**

Prepositions of Direction: *To, Away From, On (to), Off (of), In (to), Out Of*

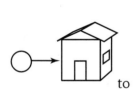
to

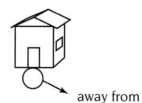
away from

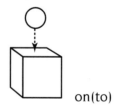
on(to)

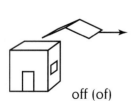
off (of)

in(to)

out of

EXAMPLES	EXPLANATIONS
(a) He gets **in (to)** the car. **(b)** He gets **on** the bus. **(c)** He gets **out of** the taxi. **(d)** He gets **off** the train.	Prepositions of direction show movement. For cars, taxis, and vans, use *in (to)* and *out of*. For buses, trains and planes, use *on (to)* and *off (of)*.

EXERCISE 6

Here is a story about the hard life of a mouse. Fill in the blanks with a preposition of direction from Focus 4.

1. The mouse comes _____ his hole.

2. The cat jumps _____ the table.

3. The mouse runs _____ the cheese.

4. The cat jumps _____ the table and runs after the mouse.

5. The cat runs _____ the mouse.

6. The mouse runs _____ his hole.

Prepositions of Direction:
Up, Down, Across, Along, Around, Over, Through, Past

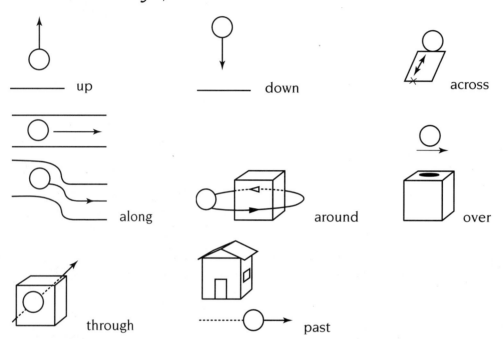

——————— up

——— down

across

along

around

over

through

past

EXERCISE 7

Here is a story about the hard life of a cat. Fill in the blanks with a preposition of direction from Focus 5.

1. The cat sees the dog. He runs _____ the field.

2. He runs _____ the grass.

3. He runs _____ the bridge.

4. He climbs _____ the tree.

5. The dog barks. He runs _____ the tree.

6. The dog's owner arrives and puts a leash on the dog. The cat climbs _____ from the tree.

7. The cat walks _____ the dog.

8. He walks _____ the road with a smile on his face.

FOCUS 6 ➤➤➤➤➤➤➤➤➤➤➤➤➤➤➤➤➤➤➤➤➤➤➤➤ **USE**

Giving Directions

Look at the map below and read the conversation on the following page.

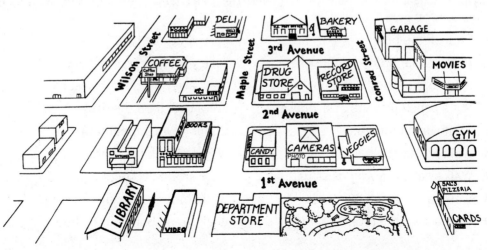

(Person A is at the bakery.)

A: Excuse me, how do I get to the department store?

B: Walk **down** Conrad Street until you get to First Avenue. Then turn **right** at the corner. Go **straight**. Walk one block. The department store is on the corner on the left.

EXERCISE 8

Look at the map in Focus 6. Follow the directions. Then answer the questions.

EXAMPLE: You are at the record store on the corner of Second Avenue and Conrad Street. Walk down Conrad Street until you get to Third Avenue. Turn left at the corner. Walk one block. Cross Third Avenue. This place is on the right. Where are you? Answer: *At the Post Office*.

1. You are at the bakery. Walk down Conrad Street and make a right on Second Avenue. Go straight and make a left on Maple Street. Walk across the street. Where are you? _____

2. You are coming out of the coffee shop entrance on Second Avenue. Walk down Second Avenue and go two blocks. Turn right on Conrad Street. Go straight until you get to First Avenue. Make a left. Walk into the building on your right. Where are you? _____

3. You are at the library on First Avenue. Walk up Wilson Street. Make a right on Third Avenue. Go straight for two blocks. Then make a left on Conrad Street. Go across the street from the bakery. Where are you? _____

EXERCISE 9

Work with a partner. Take turns giving the commands. Your partner acts out the commands you give.

1. Step off the bus.	Step onto the bus.
2. Put your hand into your pocket.	Take your hand out of your pocket.
3. Walk to the blackboard.	Walk away from the blackboard.
4. Put a pencil into the desk drawer.	Put a pencil on the desk.
5. Climb up a mountain.	Climb down a mountain.
6. Walk on the grass.	Walk through tall grass.
7. Walk away from your classmate.	Walk around your classmate.
8. Walk past a group of people.	Walk through a group of people.
9. Walk across the room.	Walk over a book on the floor.

Activities

ACTIVITY 1

DO'S AND DON'TS

STEP ❶ Make a list of do's and don'ts for someone who plans to travel to your country.

EXAMPLE: Korea

	Do's	Don'ts
Hand and body movements	Bow to say goodbye.	Don't touch or pat a man on the back—only if you are very good friends.
Eating		
Manners for a guest at a person's house		
Other		

STEP ❷ Make an oral presentation of the do's and don'ts to your class.

ACTIVITY 2

PROBLEMS AND ADVICE

STEP ❶ Work with a partner. Write down three problems you have.

STEP ❷ Tell your partner your problems.

STEP ❸ Your partner gives you advice.

EXAMPLE: You: I can't sleep at night.

Your Partner: Drink a cup of hot milk.

Problems	Advice
1.	
2.	
3.	

ACTIVITY 3

Work in a group. Create an information booklet to give advice to new students in the United States. Choose from the ideas below.

- How to Learn English
- How to Find a Job
- How to Do Well in School
- How to Find an Apartment
- How to Meet People

ACTIVITY 4

DIRECTIONS GAME

STEP ❶ Work in groups of two or three. Write directions for someone to go to different parts of the building you are in (restrooms, snack bar, etc.).

> **EXAMPLE:** Go out of the room. Turn left and go to the end of the corridor. Turn right. It's on the right.

STEP ❷ Ask the rest of the class to find out where your group is directing someone.

ACTIVITY 5

Look around your neighborhood or your home. Find imperatives in public notices. Discuss the meaning of the notices.

ACTIVITY 6

REMEDIES

 STEP ❶ Listen to the three different remedies. Match the remedy to one of the titles below.

Remedies

(a) _____ How to cure a headache

(b) _____ How to cure a cold

(c) _____ How to treat a burn

STEP ❷ Describe a remedy you know.

UNIT

Quantifiers

Who Eats a Healthy Breakfast?

The chart on page 162 shows the number of **calories** and the amount of **fat** and **cholesterol** in the foods Billy, Juanita, and Brad eat for breakfast every day.

Calories are the amount of energy a food produces in the body. To lose weight, we need to reduce our calories.

There is **fat** in foods like butter, cheese, and meat. Too much fat is bad for your health.

There is **cholesterol** in foods like eggs, butter, and cheese. Too much cholesterol can give you heart disease.

STEP ❶ Look at the chart and answer the questions.

	Calories	Fat (grams)	Cholesterol (milligrams)
Billy			
eggs (3)	140	9.8	399
sausages (2)	180	16.3	48
muffin	170	4.6	9
milk	165	8	30
Brad			
cereal	80	1.1	0
orange juice	80	0	0
nonfat milk	85	0	0
banana (1)	130	less than 1	0
Juanita			
pancakes (3)	410	9.2	21
vanilla milkshake	290	13	10
doughnuts (2)	240	20	18

1. Is there a lot of fat in Juanita's breakfast?
2. Who eats a breakfast with only a little fat?
3. Whose breakfast has a lot of calories?
4. Are there any calories in Brad's breakfast?
5. How much cholesterol is there in each breakfast?
6. Which foods don't have any cholesterol?
7. Which foods have little fat?
8. Which food has a lot of cholesterol?

STEP ❷ Whose breakfast is healthy? Write three sentences to explain why.

_____ has a healthy breakfast.

1. _____ calories

2. _____ fat.

3. _____ cholesterol.

FOCUS 1 >>>>>>>>>>>>>>>>>>>>>>>>>> **FORM**

Review of Count and Noncount Nouns

EXAMPLES	EXPLANATIONS
	Count nouns:
(a) Billy eats a **muffin** and an **egg.**	• can have *a/an* in front of them.
(b) Brad likes **pancakes.**	• can have plural forms.
(c) Billy eats three **eggs.**	• can have a number in front of them.
(d) There is a **fast-food restaurant** near here.	• can take singular or plural verbs.
(e) There are a lot of **calories** in a **milkshake.**	
(f) How many **eggs** does Billy eat?	• can be in questions with *how many.*
	Noncount nouns:
(g) Cereal is healthy.	• can't have *a/an* in front of them.
(h) He eats **bread** and **butter.**	• can't have plural forms.
(i) It has a little **cholesterol.**	• can't have a number in front of them.
(j) Nonfat **milk** is good for you.	• can't take plural verbs.
(k) How much **cholesterol** does an egg have?	• can be in questions with *how much.*

EXERCISE 1

Go back to the Opening Task on page 162. Make a list of the count and noncount nouns.

Count Nouns	Noncount Nouns
eggs	milk

Quantifiers

Quantifiers are words or phrases that show how many things or how much of something we have.

Positive Meaning

COUNT NOUNS			
	Quantifiers		
(a) There are	**many**	eggs	
(b) There are	**a lot of**	apples	in the refrigerator.
(c) There are	**some**	bananas	
(d) There are	**a few**	potatoes	
NONCOUNT NOUNS			
	Quantifiers		
(e) There is	**a lot of**	milk*	
(f) There is	**some**	juice	in the refrigerator.
(g) There is	**a little**	cake	

Negative Meaning

COUNT NOUNS			
	Quantifiers		
(h) There aren't	**many**	potatoes	
(i) There aren't	**a lot of**	potatoes	
(j) There are	**few**	tomatoes	in the refrigerator.
(k) There aren't	**any**	onions	
(l) There are	**no**	onions	
NONCOUNT NOUNS			
	Quantifiers		
(m) There isn't	**much**	cake*	
(n) There isn't	**a lot of**	cake	
(o) There is	**little**	coffee	in the refrigerator.
(p) There isn't	**any**	jam	
(q) There is	**no**	jam	

*Use *much* in negative statements. Do not use *much* in affirmative statements.

NOT: There is much milk in the refrigerator

Match the picture to the statement. Write the letter next to each statement.

Community Bank	January 31
	Account #536
Debits: $325.00	
Credits: $325.00	
	Balance: $___.00

A.

Community Bank	January 31
	Account #741
Debits: $458.31	
Credits: $958.31	
	Balance: $500.00

C.

Community Bank	January 31
	Account #289
Debits: $312.80	
Credits: $412.80	
	Balance: $100.00

B.

Community Bank	January 31
	Account #125
Debits: $ 7,096.10	
Credits: $12,096.10	
	Balance: $5,000.00

D.

_____d_____ 1. Carlos has a lot of money in the bank.

_____ 2. François has a little money in the bank.

_____ 3. Kim has no money in the bank.

_____ 4. Lee has some money in the bank.

E.

F.

G.

_____ 5. The Greens have a lot of plants in their home.

_____ 6. The Smiths don't have any plants.

_____ 7. The Taylors have a few plants.

H.

I.

J.

_____ 8. Jody has no friends.

_____ 9. Irene has a few friends.

_____ 10. Helene has a lot of friends.

K.   L.   M.

_____ 11. Bill has a lot of hair.

_____ 12. Jim doesn't have any hair.

_____ 13. Albert has a little hair.

Cross out the incorrect quantifier in each sentence.

EXAMPLE: My new apartment has ~~many~~ furniture.
                                          some
                                          a lot of

1. Middletown has   a lot of   pollution.
                           a little
                           a few

2. The teacher gives us   some   homework.
                            many
                            a little.

3. Billy has   a little   girlfriends.
                            a few
                            many

4. Mario speaks   much   languages.
                            three
                            a few

5. Majid has   a lot of   money.
                            a little
                            many

Test your knowledge about food. Check True or False. Then compare your answers to your partner's answers.

		True	False
1.	There are no calories in water.	✔	
2.	There's a lot of salt in fast food.		
3.	There are no calories in soda.		
4.	There's a lot of fat in cheese.		
5.	There are few calories in a small baked potato.		
6.	There's little cholesterol in fish.		
7.	There are few vitamins in orange juice.		
8.	There's some fat in low-fat yogurt.		
9.	There isn't any sugar in fruit.		
10.	There's a little caffeine in tea.		

Use the chart in the Opening Task on page 162 to complete the statements by adding quantifiers.

1. Doughnuts have __a lot of__ calories.

2. A banana doesn't have _____ calories.

3. There is _____ cholesterol in eggs.

4. There is _____ cholesterol in a muffin.

5. There is _____ fat in bananas.

6. Orange juice has _____ calories.

7. Sausages have _____ fat.

8. Eggs and pancakes have _____ fat.

9. There are _____ calories in cereal.

10. There is _____ cholesterol in orange juice.

11. There is _____ fat in cereal.

12. There is _____ fat in whole milk.

A Few/Few, A Little/Little

EXAMPLES	EXPLANATIONS
(a) She has **a few** books. = She has *some* books. **(b)** I have **a little** time. = I have *some* time.	A *few* and A *little* have a positive meaning. They mean *some*, or more than zero.
(c) They have **few** books. = They don't have many books. **(d)** They have **little** time. = They don't have much time.	*Few* and *Little* have a negative meaning. They mean *not much*, *not many*, almost zero.

EXERCISE 6

Linda and Kathy are both Americans living in Europe for a year. Their experiences are very different. Fill in the blanks with *few/a few* or *little/a little*.

Linda is very lonely. She doesn't have a full-time job. She has (1) __few__ friends and (2) _____ money. She works part-time as a baby sitter. She doesn't like this kind of work. She has (3) _____ patience for children. She speaks very (4) _____ Spanish.

Kathy loves to be in different countries. She speaks (5) _____ languages. She goes to a language school in Spain and she has (6) _____ very close friends. Kathy learns (7) _____ Spanish every day. She also works as a baby sitter and makes (8) _____ extra money. Kathy works hard, but she always has (9) _____ time to go out and have fun. She has (10) _____ problems in Spain.

Questions with *How Many* and *How Much*

QUESTION			ANSWER	EXPLANATIONS
How many	**Count Noun**			
(a) **How many**	universities	are there?	A lot.	Use *How many* with count nouns.
(b) **How many**	brothers	do you have?	Two.	
(c) **How many**	oranges	do you eat every day?	A few.	
How much	**Noncount Noun**			
(d) **How much**	money	do you have in your account?	$200.	Use *How much* with noncount nouns.
(e) **How much**	time	do you have?	Five minutes.	
(f) **How much**	gas	do you need?	Not much.	

EXERCISE 7

Go back to the Opening Task on page 161. Make questions with *how much* or *how many*. Then answer the questions.

1. _How many_   pancakes does Juanita usually eat for breakfast?

2. _How much_   juice does Brad drink?

3. _____ eggs does Billy have?

4. _____ cholesterol is there in three eggs?

5. _____ calories are there in a vanilla milkshake?

6. _____ cholesterol is there in a bowl of cereal?

7. _____ fat is there in two doughnuts?

8. _____ calories are there in three pancakes?

9. _____ sausages can Billy eat?

10. _____ money does Brad spend on his breakfast?

Fill in the blanks with *how much* or *how many* or a quantifier (*a lot, a little, some, any, much, many*). Then answer the questions.

1. **Mom:** How was school today, dear?

   Child: O.K., Mom . . .

   Mom: (a) _____ homework do you have tonight?

   Child: I have (b)) _____ homework—three compositions plus a spelling test tomorrow!

   Mom: Don't worry, I have (c) _____ time to help you tonight.

2. **Doctor:** Please remember to take this medicine, Mr. Josephson.

   Patient: (a) _____ medicine do I need to take every day?

   Doctor: These are pills. You need three red pills a day, one after every meal. And you need two blue pills a day, one in the morning and one before bed.

   Patient: Say that again, please . . . (b) _____ red pills?
   (c) _____ blue pills? And (d) _____ pills do I need to take in all?

   Doctor: Three red pills and two blue pills. Five pills in all. Take these for a week. Then call me.

   Patient: O.K. Thanks, Doctor.

Ask your partner questions about a city he or she knows. First ask a *yes/no* question. Then ask a question with *how many* or *how much*.

1. skyscrapers   Are there any skyscrapers in your city?
   How many skyscrapers are there?

2. crime   Is there any crime in your city?
   How much crime is there?

3. noise
4. universities
5. pollution
6. trash on the streets
7. parks
8. poor people
9. traffic
10. museums
11. beaches
12. American fast-food restaurants
13. public transportation
14. shopping malls
15. hospitals

FOCUS 5 >>>>>>>>>>>>>>>>>>>>> MEANING

Measure Words

Measure words change the way we see a thing. A measure word before a noncount noun tells us about the specific quantity.

EXAMPLE: I have a lot of coffee.   (coffee = noncount noun)

I have four cans of coffee.   (specific quantity)

a **can** of tuna a **jar** of jam a **tube** of toothpaste	a **box** of cereal a **bottle** of beer a **bag** of sugar	Containers
a **slice** of pizza a **piece** of pie	a **glass** of milk a **cup** of coffee	Portions
a **cup** of flour a **pint** of ice cream a **teaspoon** of salt	a **quart** of milk a **pound** of sugar a **gallon** of water	Specific quantities
a **head** of lettuce a **sheet** of paper	a **loaf** of bread a **bar** of soap	Other
a **bag** of apples a **pound** of onions BUT: a **dozen** eggs NOT: a dozen of eggs	a **can** of beans a **box** of chocolates **five thousand** people NOT: five thousand of people	Measure words can also be used with count nouns.

Quantifiers   **171**

Here is Maggie at the checkout counter. Write down her shopping list. Use measure words in the list.

Shopping List

a pound of	coffee	_____	oil
_____	milk	_____	soda
_____	rice	_____	bread
_____	soup	_____	soap
_____	toothpaste	_____	lettuce
_____	candy	_____	toilet paper
_____	eggs	_____	beef
_____	butter	_____	peanut butter

How much food do you have at home? Use measure words to tell your classmate what you have.

EXAMPLE: I have a quart of milk.

Correct the mistakes in the following sentences.

1. **Jane:** Can I talk to you for a minute?

   Kevin: Sure, I have little time.

2. John has much friends.

3. How many money do you have?

4. My teacher gives us many homeworks.

5. Her hairs are black.

6. Elsie is in great shape. She runs few miles a day.

7. We don't sell no newspapers here.

8. There are much stores in this city.

9. I would like some informations please.

10. My best friend gives me many advices.

11. This school has little students.

12. We have few time to finish this book.

Activities

FOOD HABIT SURVEY

Ask three students questions with *how much* and *how many* to complete the chart.

EXAMPLES: How much coffee do you drink a day?

I drink three cups a day.

How much sugar do you put in your coffee?

Two teaspoons.

	Student 1	Student 2	Student 3
1. coffee or tea/drink/a day			
2. sugar/put in coffee or tea			
3. meat/eat/a week			
4. fish/eat/a week			
5. soda/drink/a day			
6. money/spend on food/a week			
7. bread/eat/a day			
8. fruit/eat/a day			
9. salt/put on food			
10. water/drink/a day			
11. eggs/eat/a week			
12. meals/have/a day			
13. other			
14. other			

Play a circle game with all the students in the class. Make a statement starting with "I want to buy . . ." One student says an item that begins with the letter A and uses a measure word. The second student repeats the statement and adds a second item that starts with the letter B. The third student does the same and adds on an item with the letter C and so on.

EXAMPLE: **Student 1:** I want to buy a bag of apples.

Student 2: I want to buy a bag of apples and a loaf of bread.

Student 3: I want to buy a bag of apples, a loaf of bread, and a head of cabbage.

ACTIVITY 3

Choose a recipe you like and write the ingredients without writing the quantity. The other students ask you questions with *how much* and *how many* to fill in the exact quantity. Make a book of the class's favorite recipes.

EXAMPLE: Recipe: *Italian Tomato Sauce*

Ingredients: tomatoes

onions

garlic

oil

salt and pepper

Questions: How many tomatoes do you use?

How many onions do you use?

How much garlic is there?

How much oil do you use?

How much salt do you need?

ACTIVITY 4

Go to a supermarket. Look at three food labels. Write down the nutrition facts on the next page.

Nutrition Facts
Serving Size 1 Container

Amount Per Serving	
Calories 170	Calories from Fat 15

	% Daily Value*
Total Fat 2g	3%
Saturated Fat 1g	5%
Cholesterol 10mg	3%
Sodium 110mg	4%
Total Carbohydrate 31g	10%
Dietary Fiber 0g	0%
Sugars 28g	
Protein 7g	

Vitamin A 2%	•	Vitamin C	6%
Calcium 25%	•	Iron	2%

*Percent Daily Values are based on a 2,000 calorie diet.

	Example	Label 1	Label 2	Label 3
Calories per serving	120			
Fat	2g			
Cholesterol	10 mg			
Sodium	110 mg			
Sugars	28g			
Protein	7g			

Tell the class about the foods. Are they healthy or not?

ACTIVITY 5

Make your own health survey like the one in Exercise 4. Write five true statements and five false statements about calories, cholesterol, fat, and salt (sodium) in different foods. Read your statements aloud. Your partner says if the statement is True or False.

EXAMPLES: There are a lot of calories in a steak.   False

There's a little cholesterol in cheese.   False

There isn't any fat in a carrot.   True

ACTIVITY 6

Sara is calling a supermarket. She has a shopping order.

STEP ❶ Listen to her order and check the things she wants.

STEP ❷ Listen again. Write the amount she wants.

_____onions	_____potatoes	_____carrots
_____milk	_____water	_____yogurt
_____lettuce	_____cabbage	_____tomatoes
_____tuna	_____eggs	_____oil

UNIT

12

Adverbs of Manner

Does Bill Rogers Get Life Insurance?

STEP ❶ You work for a life insurance company. Look at Bill Rogers' record and read the sentences below. Check True, False, or I Don't Know.

Long Life Insurance Company
Health and Accident Record

Name:	Bill Rogers	*Sex:*	Male
Date of Birth:	9/20/58	*Marital Status:*	Single
Height:	5'7"	*Weight:*	225 pounds
Health Information:	Heart problems		
	Smokes 2 packs a day		

Offenses: Ticket for speeding: 5/19/92, 8/15/96

Not stopping at a red light: 7/14/89, 9/21/93, 12/31/94, 7/4/95

Drunk driving: 12/31/95

Crashing into a wall: 3/17/96

	True	False	I Don't Know
1. Bill is a careful driver.			
2. He eats moderately.			
3. He drives slowly.			
4. He's a heavy drinker.			
5. He works hard.			
6. He drives carefully.			
7. He is a big eater.			
8. He drives fast.			
9. He dresses neatly.			
10. He is a heavy smoker.			

STEP ❷ Work with a group. Are you going to give Bill Rogers life insurance? Tell why or why not.

Adverbs of Manner

EXAMPLES	EXPLANATIONS
(a) He is a **careful** driver.	*Careful* is an adjective. It describes the noun *driver*. The adjective goes before the noun.
(b) He drives **carefully.**	*Carefully* is an adverb of manner. It describes the verb *drive*. The adverb answers the question "how?" The adverb goes after the verb.
(c) He drives his car **carefully.** NOT: He drives carefully his car.	When there is an object after the verb, the adverb goes after the object (*his car*).

EXERCISE 1

Go back to the Opening Task on page 178. Underline all the adjectives and circle all the adverbs of manner.

EXAMPLE: Bill is a <u>careful</u> driver.

He eats (moderately.)

Spelling of Adverbs of Manner

ADJECTIVE	ADVERB	RULE
slow beautiful	slowly beautifully	Add -*ly*.
heavy	heavily	Adjectives that end in -*y*: change *y* to *i* and add -*ly*.
fantastic	fantastically	Adjectives that end with -*ic*: add -*ally*.
terrible	terribly	Adjectives that end with -*le*: drop the -*e*, and add -*y*.

EXAMPLES		EXPLANATIONS
(a) She's a **fast** driver.	**(b)** She drives **fast**.	Some adverbs have the same form as adjectives.
(c) We have an **early** dinner.	**(d)** We have dinner **early**.	
(e) We eat a **late** lunch.	**(f)** We eat lunch **late**.	
(g) We are **hard** workers.	**(h)** We work **hard**.	
(i) Joel's a **good** cook.	**(j)** He cooks **well**.	Some adverbs are irregular.
(k) He works **hard**.		Do not confuse *hard* with *hardly*. In example (l), *hardly* means "he doesn't work very much."
(l) He **hardly** works.		
(m) She is lovely.		Some words that end in -*ly* are not adverbs. They are adjectives.
(n) Marco is lonely.		
(o) That dress is ugly.		
(p) Maria is friendly.		
(q) The party is lively.		

Find three sentences that describe each occupation. Write the letters next to the occupation.

Occupations

1. I am a teacher.   _c_

       _____

2. I am a lawyer.   _____

       _____

       _____

3. I am an artist.   _____

       _____

       _____

4. I am a Secretary for the United Nations.   _____

       _____

       _____

5. I am an emergency medical technician in an ambulance.   _____

       _____

a. I respond to medical emergencies very quickly.

b. I defend my clients well.

c. I prepare lessons carefully.

d. I draw beautifully.

e. I take care of international problems urgently.

f. I give medical treatment to people carefully.

g. I paint well.

h. I speak three languages fluently.

i. I stay at the office very late.

j. I drive very fast.

k. I talk to my students politely.

l. I use colors creatively.

m. I study the law constantly.

n. I write on the blackboard neatly.

o. I act diplomatically.

How are the speakers saying the sentences below? Match each sentence with the best adverb. Write the adverb in the blank.

EXAMPLE: "Shhh, don't say a word." she said _quietly_ .

politely	sadly	nervously	quickly	shyly
incorrectly	impolitely	happily	angrily	kindly

1. "I just got engaged!" she said _____.

2. "My dog just died," he said _____.

3. "I'm in a hurry," she said _____.

4. "I ain't got no mistakes," he said _____.

5. "May I make a telephone call?" she asked _____.

6. "Bring me a menu, fast!" he said _____.

7. "This is the last time I'm telling you! Clean up your room!" she said

   _____.

8. "WWWWWWWWWWill yyyyou mmmmmmmmmarry mmmmmmmmmmme?" he
   asked _____.

9. "Please, don't ask me to speak in front of the class," she said _____.

10. "Can I help you?" he asked _____.

EXERCISE 4

Read each statement. Use the adjective in parentheses to make another statement with an adverb.

EXAMPLE: My son is a safe driver. (careful)

    My son drives carefully.

1. Baryshnikov is an excellent dancer. (graceful)

   _____

2. Uta Pippig is a great runner. (fast)

   _____

3. My father is a smoker. (heavy)

   _____

4. The President is a good speaker. (effective)

   _____

5. Pavarotti is a wonderful singer. (beautiful)

   _____

6. Teachers are hard workers. (diligent)

   _____

7. He is a careless writer. (incorrect)

   _____

8. Some children are fast learners. (quick)

   _____

9. These painters are messy workers. (sloppy)

_____

10. She is a good thinker. (quick/clear)

_____

Take turns with a partner asking and answering the questions below.

1. Why is Carrie an excellent teacher?

    (a) speak/slow

    She speaks slowly.

    (b) pronounce words/clear

    (c) prepare/careful

2. Why is Mark a good secretary?

    (a) type/fast

    (b) answer the phone/ polite

    (c) take message/accurate

3. Why is Mike a good truck driver?

    (a) drive/slow

    (b) respond/quick

    (c) work/hard

4. Why is Paula Abdul a popular performer?

    (a) sing/good
    (b) dance/fantastic

5. Why is Miyuki a good language learner?

    (a) study/hard

    (b) guess/accurate

    (c) ask questions/constant

Talking about a Person or an Action

EXAMPLES	EXPLANATIONS
(a) Isabelle Allende is a **good** writer.	When you want to say something about a person, place, or thing, use an adjective.
(b) Isabelle Allende **writes** well.	When you want to say something about a verb or action, use an adverb.
(c) She is a **very good** writer. **(d)** She writes **very well.**	You can use *very* in front of an adjective or adverb.

EXERCISE 6

Do these sentences tell us about the person or the action? Check the correct column.

	Person	Action
1. Meryl Streep is a fantastic actress.		
2. My students learn easily.		
3. Steven dances slowly.		
4. Karl's a fast runner.		
5. My children are good cooks.		
6. Bill Rogers drives carelessly.		
7. My accountant is an honest person.		
8. Marco speaks to his parents impolitely.		
9. Gloria works very hard.		
10. Our teacher is a clear speaker.		

EXERCISE 7

Read the statements on the following page. Write one sentence that tells about the person and another that tells about the action.

EXAMPLE: Can you believe it! Jeryl is the winner of the race! (runner)

She is a great runner. She runs very fast.

1. Just look at Joe! He finishes one cigarette and then starts on another. (smoker)

2. My mom cooks a great meal every night. She loves to make new dishes. (cook)

3. Gloria goes to work at 8:00 in the morning and leaves at 6:00 in the evening. She never takes a break. (worker)

4. He got another speeding ticket. This is his third ticket this year! (driver)

5. Bob can sing, dance, and play the piano too. (performer)

EXERCISE 8

Read each sentence and give three reasons why the sentence is true. Use adverbs in the reasons.

EXAMPLE: I don't want Henry to drive me downtown.

Reasons: He doesn't drive very carefully.

He drives very fast.

He's a careless driver.

1. Harold drives forty miles an hour in a sixty-five-mile-an-hour zone!
2. I can't understand Bruce when he speaks.
3. Patricia is now the chef at that expensive restaurant downtown.
4. Rose is a great secretary.
5. Lucia is a good language learner.
6. Ms. Wu is a great boss.

EXERCISE 9

Correct the mistakes in the following sentences.

1. Sarah comes to work in a suit every day. She dresses elegant.
2. Melanie speaks fluently French.

3. Sam studies three hours every night. He studies hardly.

4. Dinner starts at 8:00. They always arrive at 9:30. They always come very lately.

5. Johan plays the piano very good.

6. She speaks slow.

7. She sings lovely.

Activities

ACTIVITY 1

Work in a group. One person in the group chooses an adverb of manner, but does not tell the other students the adverb. The students in the group tell the person to do something "in that manner." The person mimes the action and the other students guess the adverb.

EXAMPLE: (First student chooses the adverb *slowly*.)

Students in the group say: "Walk to the door in that manner."

Students in the group guess: *slowly*

(Example adverbs: *slowly, fast, nervously, happily, angrily, loudly, sadly, romantically*.)

ACTIVITY 2

Work in a group. Are you a good student? A good mother? A good friend? A good worker? Choose one and tell your group five reasons to explain why or why not. Use adverbs of manner.

ACTIVITY 3

Think about the Opening Task on page 177–178. Interview your partner. Role-play a conversation between an insurance agent and a person like Bill Rogers. The person tries to convince the agent to give him/her insurance. Then explain to the class why your partner can or cannot get insurance easily.

ACTIVITY 4

 STEP ❶ Listen to the three people. What are their occupations? Choose from the occupations below.

waiter   salesperson   flight attendant   doctor   receptionist

STEP ❷ Describe an occupation to the class. Use adverbs. The class guesses the occupation.

UNIT

13

Direct and Indirect Objects, Direct and Indirect Object Pronouns

OPENING TASK

Giving Gifts

You need to give a gift to the people on your list below. Look at the gifts you have and decide which gift you want to give to each person.

Gifts

A. Camera

B. Flowers

C. Toaster

D. Doll

E. Earrings

F. Running Shoes

G. Compact Disc Player

People

1. a single thirty-five-year-old athletic male friend
2. your sixty-three-year-old grandmother
3. your friend's four-year-old daughter
4. an artistic twenty-seven-year-old friend
5. your mother
6. your music-loving boyfriend/girlfriend
7. a newlywed couple

Direct Objects

EXAMPLES			EXPLANATIONS
Subject	**Verb**	**Direct Object**	
(a) My friend	sings.		Some sentences have only a subject and a verb.
(b) He	loves	music.	Some sentences have a subject, a verb, and an object.
(c) He	buys	compact discs.	A direct object answers the question "What?" *Compact discs* is the direct object.
(d) He	loves	the Beatles.	A direct object also can answer the question "Who(m)?" *The Beatles* is the direct object.

EXERCISE 1

Underline the direct object in each sentence below.

EXAMPLE: My friend loves <u>sports</u>.

1. My grandmother loves flowers. She always has fresh flowers on the dining room table.
2. Andrea and Bob have a new home.
3. My mother adores jewelry.
4. My friend's daughter has a doll collection. She owns ten different dolls.
5. Akiko takes beautiful pictures.
6. My friend enjoys classical music. She prefers Mozart.
7. In my family, we always celebrate our birthdays together.

FOCUS 2 >>>>>>>>>>>>>>>>>>>>> FORM/USE

Direct Object Pronouns

EXAMPLES	EXPLANATIONS
Subject **Verb** **Direct Object** **(a)** My mother loves my father. **(b)** My mother loves him.	The direct object can also be a pronoun.
(c) My mother loves **my father.** She thinks about **him** all the time. **(d)** My father loves **my mother.** He thinks about **her** all the time.	Object pronouns refer to a noun that comes before. In (c), *him* refers to "my father." In (d), *her* refers to "my mother."

SUBJECT	VERB	OBJECT PRONOUN	SUBJECT	VERB	OBJECT PRONOUN
I	am				me.
You	are				you.
He	is				him.
She	is	a good person.	She	loves	her.
It	is				it.
We	are				us.
You	are				you.
They	are				them.

EXERCISE 2

Fill in the correct subject or object pronouns.

1. My grandmother is a very special person. (a) _____ has a vegetable garden in her backyard. (b) _____ plants tomatoes, cucumbers, eggplant, leeks and carrots. She picks (c) _____ fresh every day. We love her fresh vegetables. (d) _____ taste delicious. We eat (e) _____ in salads and soup. Her vegetable garden gives (f) _____ great pleasure.

190   Unit 13

2. Mariela and Juan are newlyweds. (a) _____ have a new home, and
(b) _____ really love (c) _____ . Their appliances are
on order, but they don't have (d) _____ yet, so Mariela and Juan
have a lot of work to do. He helps (e) _____ with the cooking. She
helps (f) _____ with the laundry.

3. Sally: Billy, do you like heavy metal music?

   Billy: (a) _____ (b) love _____ !

   Sally: Really? I hate heavy metal. (c) _____ bothers
   (d) _____ . I hate all that noise.

This is a story about three people in a love triangle. Maggie has a steady boyfriend,
Ted. She also has a male friend, Jim. Read the text below. Cross out the incorrect
pronouns and write the correct pronouns above them.

Maggie

Jim

Ted

Maggie loves her boyfriend, Ted. She also likes Jim. (1) Jim works with ~~she~~ *her*.

(2) She sees he every day. (3) She sometimes invites he to dinner. (4) She likes to

talk with he. (5) Maggie doesn't love Jim, but Jim loves she. (6) Jim thinks about

she all the time. Jim knows about Ted, but Ted doesn't know about Jim. Ted is very

jealous. (7) So, Maggie can't tell he about Jim. (8) Maggie doesn't want to leave he.

But she cares for both Ted and Jim. She doesn't know what to do. (9) She doesn't

want to hurt they. She says to herself, "What's wrong with me? (10) Ted loves I and

I love he. (11) Jim is my friend and I like he. So what can I do?"

Direct and Indirect Objects, Direct and Indirect Object Pronouns   **191**

Ted finds out about Jim. He talks to Maggie on the phone late one night. Fill in the correct object pronouns.

1. **Ted:** Hello, Maggie. Do you remember (a) _me_____?

   Maggie: Of course, I remember (b) _____, Ted. You're my boyfriend!

2. **Ted:** I know about Jim, Maggie.

   Maggie: What? You know about (a) _____?

3. **Ted:** That's right, Maggie. I know everything about (a) _____.

   Maggie: How do you know?

   Ted: John—your secretary—told me. I meet (b) _____ for lunch sometimes. He knows about (c) _____ and Jim.

4. **Ted:** Jim can't come between (a) _____, Maggie.

   Maggie: I know, Ted. Don't worry. I don't love (b) _____.

   We're just friends.

   Ted: Do you love (c) _____?

   Maggie: Of course, I love (d) _____, Ted. I want to marry (e) _____.

5. **Ted:** You can't see (a) _____ so much, Maggie.

   Maggie: Ted, please trust (b) _____.

Ask your partner questions with *how often*. Your partner answers with object pronouns.

EXAMPLE: You: How often do you call your parents?

      Your Partner: I call them every week.

1. clean your room?
2. do your laundry?
3. see your dentist?
4. buy the newspaper?
5. cut your nails?

6. wash your hair?
7. visit your friends?
8. drink coffee?
9. do the grocery shopping?
10. watch the news?

Indirect Objects

	EXAMPLES			EXPLANATIONS
Subject	**Verb**	**Direct Object**	**Indirect Object**	
(a) I	want to give	the toaster	to **the newlyweds.**	Some sentences have two objects: a direct object and an indirect object. *The toaster* is the direct object. It tells **what** I want to give. *The newlyweds* is the indirect object. It tells to **whom** I give the toaster.
(b) I	buy	flowers	for **my grand-mother.**	*My grandmother* is the indirect object. It tells for **whom** I buy flowers.
(c) I	want to give	the toaster	to **the newlyweds.**	The indirect object can be a noun or a pronoun.
(d) I	want to give	the toaster	to **them.**	

EXAMPLES	EXPLANATIONS
(e) I fix the car **for** my grandmother.	**For and To** *For* tells us one person does the action to help or please another person.
(f) I give earrings **to** my mother.	*To* tells us about direction of the action: The earrings go from you to your mother.

Write sentences telling what you want to give to each of the people in the Opening Task. Underline the direct object and circle the indirect object. Then tell why you want to give that item to that person.

EXAMPLE: I want to give <u>the toaster</u> to the (newlyweds.) They have a new home and don't have any appliances.

New Year's Resolutions. Every January 1st, North Americans decide to change their lives and do things differently. Read the resolutions below. Change each underlined noun to a pronoun. Then add the information in parentheses.

EXAMPLE: Every year, I give <u>my father</u> a tie. (golf clubs)

This year, I want to give him golf clubs.

1. Used car salesman:

   I always sell <u>my customers</u> bad cars. (good cars)

   This year, I want to . . .

2. Child away at college:

   I always write to <u>my parents</u> once a month. (once a week)

   This year, I want to . . .

3. People with money problems:

   Every year, the bank sends <u>my husband and me</u> a big credit card bill. (a very small bill)

   This year, I want the bank to . . .

4. Boyfriend:

   I usually buy <u>my girlfriend</u> flowers for her birthday. (a diamond ring)

   This year, I want to . . .

5. Teenager:

   Sometimes I lie to <u>my mother</u>. (tell the truth)

   This year, I want to . . .

6. Mother:

   I never have time to read to <u>my children</u> at night. (every night)

   This year, I want to . . .

7. Student:

I always give my homework to <u>the teacher</u> late. (on time)

This semester, I want to . . .

8. Friend:

Every year, I lend money to <u>you and your brother</u>. (lend money)

This year, I don't want to . . .

Now say three things you want to do differently this year.

FOCUS 4 >>>>>>>>>>>>>>>>>>>>>>>>>>> FORM

Position of the Indirect Object

All verbs that take indirect objects can follow Pattern A.

Pattern A

SUBJECT	VERB	DIRECT OBJECT	INDIRECT OBJECT
(a) I	give	presents	to my mother on her birthday.
(b) I	give	presents	to her.
(c) I	give	them	to her.
(d) We	have	a party	for our twin daughters on their birthday.
(e) We	have	a party	for them.
(f) We	have	it	for them.

Some of these verbs also follow Pattern B. In Pattern B, put the indirect object before the direct object. Do not use *to* or *for*.

Pattern B

SUBJECT	VERB	INDIRECT OBJECT	DIRECT OBJECT
(g) People	send	their friends	birthday cards.
(h) People	send	them	birthday cards.
(i) I	make	my friends	birthday cakes.
(j) I	make	them	birthday cakes.

NOTE: Do not put an indirect object pronoun before a direct object pronoun.

I make my friend a cake.

I make her a cake.

NOT: I make her it.

Verbs that follow both Pattern A and B

give	send	pass	mail	make	do (a favor)
write	bring	read	offer	buy	find
show	hand	lend	pay	bake	get
tell	sell	teach	throw	cook	

EXERCISE 8

Work with a partner and make sentences about North American customs with the words below.

BIRTH: When a baby is born:

1. mother / flowers / the / to / give / friends

   Friends give flowers to the mother.

2. cigars / gives / friends / father / his / the

3. send / and / parents / friends / family / to / birth / announcements / their / the

4. baby / family / friends / gifts / the / buy / and

5. make / for / grandmothers / sweaters / new / the / baby

6. grandfathers / for / toys / make / baby / the

7. child / the / the / parents / everything / give

ENGAGEMENT/MARRIAGE: When a couple gets engaged or married:

8. diamond / man / a / woman / the / gives / ring / the / to / sometimes

9. friends / couple / an / party / the / for / have / engagement

10. gifts / woman / give / friends / at a party / the

11. at the wedding / to / couple / gifts / give / guests / the

DEATH: When someone dies:

12. send / family / some / flowers / people / the

13. people / special cards / the / send / family / to

14. some / to / give / people / money / charities

15. some / food / for / family / bring / people / the

FOCUS 5 >>>>>>>>>>>>>>>>>>>>>>>>> USE

Position of New Information

New information in a sentence comes at the end. You can write a sentence in two different ways. Both are correct, but the emphasis is different.

EXAMPLES	EXPLANATIONS
(a) Whom do you give earrings to? I usually give earrings to **my mother.**	The emphasis is on **who(m).** My *mother* is the new information.
(b) What do you usually give your mother? I usually give my mother **earrings.**	The emphasis is on **what.** E*arrings* is the new information.

EXERCISE 9

Answer the following question. The new information is in parentheses ( ).

EXAMPLES: Who(m) do you usually give presents to at Christmas? (my family)

I usually give presents to my family.

What do you usually give your father? (a good book)

I usually give him a good book.

1. Who(m) do you want to give a present to at work? (three of my co-workers)

2. What do you usually give your parents for their anniversary? (tickets to a play)

3. Who(m) do you tell jokes to? (my friend)

4. What do you sometimes send your sister? (some new recipes)

5. Does she teach English to your brother or sister? (my brother)

6. Which story do you usually read to your little sister—"Cinderella" or "Snow White"? ("Cinderella")

7. Who(m) do you need to mail the application to? (the admissions office)

8. What do you usually buy for your son on his birthday? (compact discs)

EXERCISE 10

Choose the best sentence.

EXAMPLE: You are waiting for a friend in front of a restaurant.

You do not have your watch. You want to know the time.

You see someone coming. You ask him:

(a) Could you please tell me the time?

(b) Could you please tell the time to me?

1. You are alone at a restaurant. You finish your meal. You see the waiter. You ask him:

   (a) Could you please give the check to me?

   (b) Could you please give me the check?

2. You are celebrating someone's birthday with a group of friends. You finish your meal. You want to be sure you pay the check. You tell the waiter:

   (a) Please give the check to me.

   (b) Please give me the check.

3. What do your children usually do for you on Mother's Day?

   (a) They usually serve breakfast in bed to me.

   (b) They usually serve me breakfast in bed.

4. You are at a friend's house for dinner. The food needs salt. You say:

   (a) Please pass me the salt.

   (b) Please pass the salt to me.

5. You realize you don't have any money on you for the bus. You ask a friend:

    (a) Could you lend a dollar to me?

    (b) Could you lend me a dollar?

6. You are in class. It is very noisy. You say to a classmate:

    (a) Do me a favor. Please close the door.

    (b) Do a favor for me. Please close the door.

7. Why does your class look so sad on Mondays?

    (a) because our teacher gives us a lot of homework.

    (b) because our teacher gives a lot of homework to us.

8. You are speaking to the Director of the English Language Institute. You want to apply to the City University. You have the application form in your hand.

    Director: (a) Please send the application form to the City University.

    (b) Please send the City University the application form.

9. You come home from the supermarket. Your car is full of groceries. You need help. You say to your roommate:

    (a) Can you please give a hand to me?

    (b) Can you please give me a hand?

10. There are three children at a table. They are finishing a box of cookies. A fourth child sees them and runs toward them. The child says:

    (a) Wait! Save me one!

    (b) Wait! Save one for me!

FOCUS 6

Verbs that Do Not Omit *To* with Indirect Objects

EXAMPLES	EXPLANATIONS
S + V + DO + IO **(a)** My mother reads stories to us. **S + V + IO + DO** **(b)** My mother reads us stories.	Many verbs follow both Pattern A and B. (See Focus 4.)
DO + IO **(c)** The teacher explains the grammar to us. **(d)** NOT: The teacher explains us the grammar.	Some verbs only follow Pattern A.
explain *describe* *repeat* *introduce* *report* *say* *solve* *open* *carry* *clean* *do* *prepare* *fix* *repair* *spell*	Verbs that follow Pattern A ONLY. Do not omit *to/for*.

EXERCISE 11

Read the following pairs of sentences or questions aloud. Check any sentence that is not possible. In some pairs, both patterns are possible.

EXAMPLE 1:

Pattern A: My husband sends flowers to me every Valentine's Day.

Pattern B: My husband sends me flowers every Valentine's Day.

(Both patterns are possible.)

EXAMPLE 2:

Pattern A: The teacher always repeats the question to the class.

NOT: **Pattern B:** The teacher always repeats the class the question.

Pattern A	Pattern B
1. Tell the truth to me.	Tell me the truth.
2. Please explain the problem to me.	Please explain me the problem.
3. Spell that word for me, please.	Spell me that word, please.
4. I need to report the accident to the insurance company.	I need to report the insurance company the accident.
5. My father usually reads a story to my little brother every night.	My father usually reads my little brother a story every night.
6. He always opens the door for me.	He always opens me the door.
7. Let me introduce my friend to you.	Let me introduce you my friend.
8. Cynthia gives her old clothes to a charity.	Cynthia gives a charity her old clothes.
9. The students write letters to their parents every week.	The students write their parents letters every week.
10. Please repeat the instructions to the class.	Please repeat the class the instructions.
11. Can you describe your hometown to me?	Can you describe me your hometown?
12. Can you carry that bag for me?	Can you carry me that bag?

Activities

ACTIVITY 1

Think of the different things people have. Then give clues so that your classmates can guess the object.

EXAMPLE: Clues: The Japanese make a lot of them. We drive them. What are they?

Answer: Cars!

ACTIVITY 2

STEP ❶ Write down the names of ten occupations on ten pieces of paper.

STEP ❷ Choose one of the pieces of paper and make sentences for the class so they can guess the profession. You get one point for each sentence you make.

STEP ❸ When the class guesses the profession, another student picks a piece of paper. The person with the most points at the end wins.

> **EXAMPLE:** (You choose "firefighter.")
>
> > **You say:** *This person wears a hat.*
> >
> > *He or she drives a big vehicle.*
> >
> > *He or she saves people's lives.*

ACTIVITY 3

STEP ❶ Each person in the class writes down a personal habit—good or bad.

STEP ❷ Each person reads his or her statement to the class.

STEP ❸ The class asks questions to find out more information.
(Possible habits: playing with your hair, tapping your feet.)

> **EXAMPLE: You:** *I bite my fingernails.*
>
> **Class:** *Why do you bite them?*
>
> **You:** *Because I'm nervous!*

ACTIVITY 4

What customs do you have in your country for events such as birth, engagement, marriage, death? Tell the class what people do in your country.

> **EXAMPLE:** In Chile, when a baby is born . . .
>
> > when a couple gets married . . .
> >
> > when someone dies . . .
> >
> > when a person turns thirteen . . .
> >
> > OTHER . . .

Work in a small group. On small slips of paper, write the numbers 1 to 16 and put them in an envelope. One person in the class is the "caller" and only he or she looks at the grid below. The first student picks a number from the envelope. The caller calls out the command in that square for the student to follow. Then a second student picks out a number and the caller calls out the command. Continue until all the commands are given.

EXAMPLE: You pick the number 7.

Caller: Lend some money to Maria.

1. Whisper a secret to the person across from you.	2. Give a penny to the person on your left.	3. Write a funny message to someone in your group.	4. Hand your wallet to the person on your right.
5. Make a paper airplane for the person across from you.	6. Tell a funny joke to someone.	7. Lend some money to a person in your group.	8. Describe a friend to someone.
9. Explain indirect objects to the person across from you.	10. Tell your age to the person on your right.	11. Introduce the person on your left to the person on your right.	12. Offer candy to someone.
13. Call up the police and report a crime to them.	14. Open the door for someone in the class.	15. Throw your pen to the person across from you.	16. Pass a secret message to one person in your group.

STEP ❶ Listen to the conversation between Linda and Amy. Then read the statements below. Check True or False.

	True	False
1. Linda is giving her mother perfume on Mother's Day.		
2. Linda's mother tells her what gift she wants.		
3. Amy's mother always tells her daughter what gift she wants.		
4. Linda's father only takes Linda's mother to a restaurant on Mother's Day.		
5. Linda's father does not buy his wife a gift.		

STEP ❷ Work with a partner. If a statement is false, make a true statement.

STEP ❸ Tell your classmates what you do and give to a person on a special day like Mother's Day or a birthday.

Appendices

APPENDIX 1   FORMING VERB TENSES

Appendix 1A   *Be*: Present Tense

I	am	
He She It	is	from Japan.
We You They	are	
There	is	a student from Japan.
There	are	students from all over the world in this class.

Appendix 1B   *Be*: Past Tense

I He She It	was	happy.
We You They	were	
There	was	a party yesterday.
There	were	a lot of people there.

Appendix 1C   Simple Present

I You We They	work.
He She It	works.

Appendix 1D   Present Progressive

I	am	
He She It	is	working.
We You They	are	

Appendix 1E   Simple Past

I He She It We You They	worked	yesterday.

Appendix 1F   Future Tense with *Will*

I He She It We You They	will work	tomorrow.

Appendix 1G   Future Tense with *Be Going To*

I	am	
He She It	is	going to work in a few minutes.
We You They	are	

Appendix 1H   *Can/Might/May*

I He She It We You They	can might may	work.

Appendix 1I   *Be Able To*

I	am	
He She It	is	able to dance.
We You They	are	

Appendix 2A   Plural Nouns

Nouns	Singular	Plural
Regular	book	books
	table	tables
Ends in vowel + *y*	toy	toys
Ends in vowel + *o*	radio	radios
Ends in consonant + *o*	potato	potatoes
	tomato	tomatoes
Ends in -*y*	city	cities
Ends in *f*, *fe*	thief	thieves
	wife	wives
(Except)	chief	chiefs
	chef	chefs
Ends in *ss*, *ch*, *sh*, *x*, and *z*	class	classes
	sandwich	sandwiches
	dish	dishes
	box	boxes
Irregular plural nouns	man	men
	woman	women
	child	children
	person	people
	foot	feet
	tooth	teeth
	mouse	mice
Plurals that stay the same	sheep	sheep
	deer	deer
	fish	fish
No singular form		scissors
		pants
		shorts
		pajamas
		glasses
		clothes

Appendix 2B   Simple Present: Third Person Singular

Rule	Example
1. Add -s to form the third person singular of most verbs.	My brother **sleeps** 8 hours a night
2. Add -es to verbs ending in sh, ch, x, z, or ss.	She **watches** television every evening.
3. When the verb ends in a consonant + y, change the y to i and add -es.	He **hurries** to class every morning.
4. When the verb ends in a vowel + y, do not change the y. Add -s.	My sister **plays** the violin.
5. Irregular Forms: have go do	He **has** a good job. He **goes** to work every day. He **does** the laundry.

Appendix 2C   Present Progressive

Rule		
1. Add -ing to the base form of the verb.	talk study do agree	talking studying doing agreeing
2. If the verb ends in a single -e, drop the -e and add -ing.	drive	driving
3. If a one-syllable verb ends in a consonant, a vowel, and a consonant (c-v-c), double the last consonant and add -ing.	(c-v-c) s i t r u n	sitting running
Do not double the consonant, if the verb ends in w, x, or y.	s h o w f i x p l a y	showing fixing playing
4. In two-syllable verbs that end in a consonant, a vowel, and a consonant (c-v-c), double the last consonant only if the last syllable is stressed.	beGIN LISten	beginning listening
5. If the verb ends in -ie, drop the -ie, add -y and -ing.	lie die	lying dying

Appendix 2D   Simple Past of Regular Verbs

Rule		
1. Add *-ed* to most regular verbs.	start	started
2. If the verb ends in an *-e*, add *-d*.	like	liked
3. If the verb ends in a consonant + *y*, change the *y* to *i* and add *-ed*.	study	studied
4. If the verb ends in a vowel + *y*, don't change the *y* to *i*. Add *-ed*.	enjoy play	enjoyed played
5. If a one-syllable verb ends in a consonant, a vowel, and a consonant (c-v-c), double the last consonant and add *-ed*.	stop	stopped
Do not double the last consonant if it is *w, x,* or *y*.	show fix play	showed fixed played
6. If a two-syllable word ends in a consonant, a vowel, and a consonant (c-v-c), double the last consonant if the stress is on the last syllable.	ocCUR LISten	occurred listened

APPENDIX 3   PRONUNCIATION RULES

Appendix 3A   Regular Plural Nouns

/s/	/z/		/ɪz/
After voiceless sounds (*f, k, p, t, th*)	After voiced sounds (*b, d, g, l, m, n, r, v, ng,* and vowel sounds)		After *s, z, sh, ch, ge/dge* sounds. (This adds another syllable to the word.)
cuffs	jobs	pens	classes
books	beds	cars	exercises
maps	rugs	leaves	dishes
pots	schools	rings	sandwiches
months	rooms	days	colleges

Appendix 3B   Simple Present Tense: Third Person Singular

/s/	/z/	/ɪz/
After voiceless sounds (*p, t, f, k*)	After voiced final sounds (*b, d, v, g, l, m, n, r, ng*)	Verbs ending in sh, ch, x, z, ss. (This adds another syllable to the word.)
He sleeps. She works.	She drives a car. He prepares dinner.	He teaches English She rushes to class.

Appendix 3C   Simple Past Tense of Regular Verbs

/t/	/d/	/ɪd/
After voiceless sounds (*s, k, p, f, sh, ch, x*)	After voiced final sounds (*b, g, l, m, n, r, v, x*)	Verbs ending in *t* or *d*. (This adds another syllable to the word.)
He kissed her once. She asked a question.	We learned a song. They waved goodbye.	She painted a picture. The plane landed safely.

APPENDIX 4   TIME EXPRESSIONS

Appendix 4A   Simple Present

Adverbs of Frequency	Frequency Expressions	Time Expressions
always often frequently usually sometimes seldom rarely never	every { morning afternoon night summer winter spring fall day week year } all the time once a week twice a month 3 times a year once in a while	in { 1997 October the fall } on { Monday Sundays January 1st the weekend } at { 6:00 noon night midnight }

Appendix 4B   Present Progressive

now	this semester
right now	this evening
at the moment	this week
today	this year
these days	

Appendix 4C   Past

yesterday	last	ago	in/on/at
yesterday { morning, afternoon, evening }	last { night, week, month, year, summer }	{ an hour, two days, 6 months, a year } ago	in { 1988, June, the evening } on { Sunday, December 1, weekends } at { 6:00, night, midnight }

Appendix 4D   Future

this	next	tomorrow	other	in/on/at
this { morning, afternoon, evening }	next { week, month, year, Sunday, weekend, summer }	tomorrow { morning, afternoon, evening, night }	soon later a week from today tonight for 3 days until 3:00	in { 15 minutes, a few days, 2 weeks, March, 2005 } on { Tuesday, May 21 } at { 4:00, midnight }

Appendix 5A   Subject Pronouns

Subject Pronouns		
I	am	
You	are	
He		
She	is	
It		happy.
We		
You	are	
They		

Appendix 5B   Object Pronouns

		Object Pronouns
		me.
		you
		him.
		her.
She	loves	it.
		us.
		you.
		them.

Appendix 5C   Demonstrative Pronouns

This	is a list of subject pronouns.
That	
These	are object pronouns.
Those	

Appendix 5D   Possessive Pronouns

This book is	mine.
	his.
	hers.
	*
	ours.
	yours.
	theirs.

*"It" does not have a possessive pronoun.

Appendix 5E   Reflexive Pronouns

I		myself.
		yourself.
We	love	ourselves.
You		yourselves.
They		themselves.
He		himself.
She	loves	herself.
It		itself.

Appendix 5F   Reciprocal Pronoun

Friends help each other.

APPENDIX 6   POSSESSIVES

Appendix 6A   Possessive Nouns

Bob's Thomas' Thomas's The teacher's The students' The children's Bob and Andrea's	house is big.

Appendix 6B   Possessive Determiners

My Your His Her Its Our Your Their	house is big.

Appendix 6C   Possessive Pronouns

	mine. your. his. hers. * ours. yours theirs.
The house is	

*"It" does not have a possessive pronoun.

COMPARISONS WITH
APPENDIX 7 | ADJECTIVES AND ADVERBS

Appendix 7A   **Comparative Form (to compare two people, places, or things)**

Betsy	is	older bigger busier later more punctual less talkative	than	Judy.
	plays the violin	faster more beautifully better		

Appendix 7B   **Superlative Form (to compare one thing or person to all the others in a group)**

Betsy	is	the oldest the biggest the busiest the most practical the least punctual	of all her sisters.
	plays the violin	the fastest the most beautifully the best	

Appendix 7C   **A/As (to say that two people, places, or things are the same)**

Betsy	is	as	old big busy practical punctual	as	Judy.
	plays the violin		fast beautifully well		

PAST-TENSE FORMS OF

COMMON IRREGULAR VERBS

Simple Form	Past-Tense Form	Past Participle	Simple Form	Past-Tense Form	Past Participle
be	was	were	leave	left	left
become	became	became	lend	lent	lent
begin	began	begun	let	let	let
bend	bent	bent	lose	lost	lost
bite	bit	bit	make	made	made
blow	blew	blown	meet	met	met
break	broke	broken	pay	paid	laid
bring	brought	brought	put	put	put
build	built	built	quit	quit	quit
buy	bought	bought	read	read*	read
catch	caught	caught	ride	rode	ridden
choose	chose	chosen	ring	rang	rung
come	came	come	run	ran	run
cost	cost	cost	say	said	said
cut	cut	cut	see	saw	seen
dig	dug	dug	sell	sold	sold
do	did	done	send	sent	sent
draw	drew	drown	shake	shook	shaken
drink	drank	drunk	shoot	shot	shot
drive	drove	driven	shut	shut	shut
eat	ate	eaten	sing	sang	sung
fall	fell	fallen	sit	sat	sat
feed	fed	fed	sleep	slept	slept
feel	felt	felt	speak	spoke	spoken
fight	fought	fought	spend	spent	spent
find	found	found	stand	stood	stood
fly	flew	flown	steal	stole	stolen
forget	forgot	forgotten	swim	swam	swum
get	got	gotten	take	took	taken
give	gave	given	teach	taught	taught
go	went	gone	tear	tore	torn
grow	grew	grown	tell	told	told
hang	hung	hung	think	thought	thought
have	had	had	throw	threw	thrown
hear	heard	heard	understand	understood	understood
hide	hid	hidden	wake	woke	woken
hit	hit	hit	wear	wore	worn
hold	held	held	win	won	won
hurt	hurt	hurt	write	wrote	written
keep	kept	kept			
know	knew	known			
lead	led	led			

* Pronounce the base form: /rid/; pronounce the past-tense form: red.

Answer Key
(for puzzles and problems only)

UNIT 17

Answers to Opening Task (page 257)

1. Martin Luther King, Jr. wasn't African;, he was African-American. He was a civil rights leader.

2. The Beatles were British. They weren't hairdressers; they were musicians.

3. Marilyn Monroe was American. She was an actress.

4. Indira Gandhi was Indian. She wasn't a rock singer; she was the prime minister of India.

5. Pierre and Marie Curie were French. They weren't fashion designers; they were scientists.

6. Mao was Chinese. He was a political leader in the People's Republic of China.

7. Jacqueline Kennedy Onassis wasn't Greek; she was American. She was the wife of John F. Kennedy, president of the United States, and later of Aristotle Onassis, who was a Greek millionaire.

8. George Washington, Thomas Jefferson, Abraham Lincoln and Theodore Roosevelt weren't Canadian, they were American. They were presidents. Their heads are on Mt. Rushmore in South Dakota.

UNIT 19

Answer to Activity 1 (page 301)

The prisoner stood on a block of ice with the rope around his neck. When the ice melted, his feet didn't touch the ground, so he hanged himself.

Exercises
(second parts)

Exercise 6 (page 21)

Chart B

Name: Age:	Cindy 22	Shelley 27	Gloria 30
1. Height			
tall			
average height		✔	
short			
2. Weight			
thin	✔		
average weight			
overweight			✔
3. Personality			
shy		✔	
friendly			
quiet		✔	
talkative			
neat		✔	✔
messy			
funny			
serious		✔	✔
nervous			
calm		✔	

Answers to Exercise 6 (page 36)

MAP B

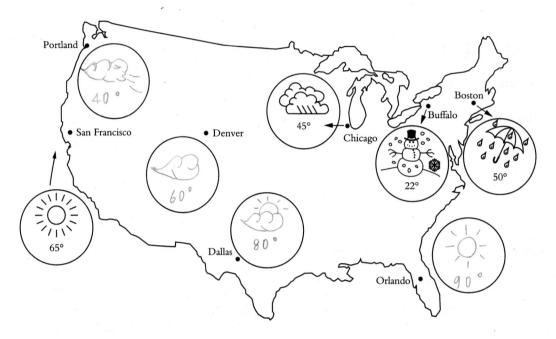

Exercise 10 (page 42)

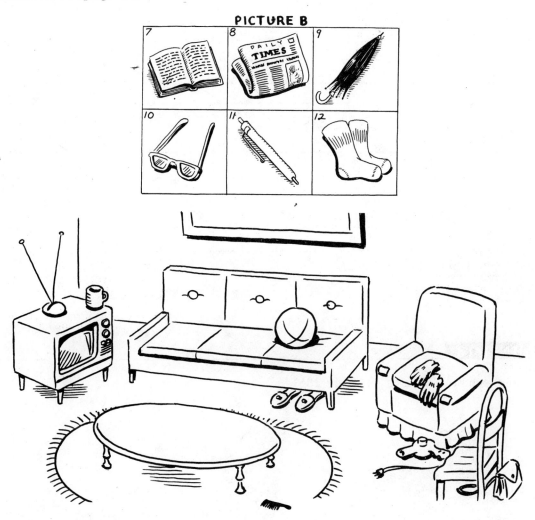

Exercise 2 (page 132)

Student B:

	Nahal		Sang-Woo	
	Yes	No	Yes	No
1. like to learn English			✔	
2. want to meet English-speaking people	✔			
3. feel nervous when speaking English			✔	
4. like to work in groups	✔			
5. need grammar rules to learn English			✔	
6. learn by speaking and listening to English	✔			
7. learn by reading and writing English			✔	
8. learn slowly, step by step		✔		
9. try new ways of learning				✔

UNIT 18

Conclusion to Exercise 12 (page 286)

Answers to Exercise 15 (page 289)

Text B

1. Doina grew up in _____ (where).

2. She married a government official.

3. She had _____ in 1976 (what).

4. Doina was unhappy _____ (why).

5. She thought of ways to escape.

6. She taught her daughter _____ (what).

7. On October 9, 1988, she and her daughter swam across the Danube River to Serbia.

8. _____ caught them (who).

9. Doina and her daughter went to jail.

10. They tried to escape _____ (when).

11. Finally, they left Romania on foot in the middle of the night.

12. They flew to _____ in 1989 (where).

13. Doina went to school to learn English.

14. She wrote _____ (what) in her ESL class.

Activity 6 (page 292)

Only the Host looks at this game board.

GAME BOARD

$$$	Category 1 PEOPLE	Category 2 WH-QUESTIONS	Category 3 YES/NO QUESTIONS
$10	Ms. Ditto.	A VCR.	Yes, she did.
$20	Harry.	On the first day of classes.	Yes, he did.
$30	The Director.	In the language lab.	No, he didn't.
$40	Professor Brown.	Because he needed pay for the ESL classes again this semester.	No, he didn't
$50	The students.	She noticed grammar mistakes in the note.	Yes, they did.

Exercise 4 (page 377)

CHART B

	North America	South America	Asia	Europe	Africa	The World
long river	The Mississippi		The Yangtze		The Nile	
large country		Brazil		France		The People's Republic of China
populated country	The United States		The People's Republic of China		Nigeria	
high mountain		Mt. Aconcagua		Mt. Elbrus		Mt. Everest
small country	Bermuda		Macao		the Seychelles	

Credits

Text Credits

Unit 8, Exercise 4: Cartoon by Sergio Aragones, from *Mad Magazine*. Reprinted by permission of Sergio Aragones.

Unit 18, Exercise 3: Cartoon by Sergio Aragones, from *Mad Magazine*. Reprinted by permission of Sergio Aragones.

Unit 18, Exercise 12, and Activity 2: Cartoon by Sergio Aragones, from *Mad Magazine*. Reprinted by permission of Sergio Aragones.

Photo Credits

Page 1: © Rob Crandall, The Image Works. Page 5: seated couple, © D. Young-Wolf, Photo Edit; student, © Michelle Bridwell, Photo Edit. Page 6: Argentinian students, © Michael Dwyer, Stock Boston; Nigerian men, © Beryl Goldberg. Page 29: Pyramids, The Bettmann Archive; Himalayan Mountains, Mark Antman, The Image Works; Fourth of July fireworks, © Archive Photos/Lambert; the Kremlin, © Bill Aaron, Photo Edit. Page 91: © Dana White, Photo Edit. Page 257: all photos, © Archive Photos. Page 258: all photos, © Archive Photos. Page 266: The Image Works. Page 303: © Archive Photos/Curry. Page 392: © Reuters/Jack Naegelen Archive Photos.

Index